How to build

A WINNING BID TEAM

Existing and planned titles in the Helping Hand book series:

How to write the perfect press release
Real-life advice from editors on getting your story in the media

How to build a winning bid team
Practical advice to improve key skills that help you win more business

How to write well at work
Simple steps to get you writing with fluency and confidence
(Published 10 April 2006)

How to sell articles to newspapers and magazines
A proven approach – from getting the idea to banking the cheque
(Published 31 May 2006)

All available from
www.helpinghandbooks.co.uk

How to build
a winning bid team

Practical advice to improve key skills
that help you win more business

CAROL KENNEDY AND PETER BARTRAM

A Helping Hand Book
from
New Venture Publishing

First published 2006 as a Helping Hand Book
by New Venture Publishing Ltd
© Carol Kennedy and Peter Bartram 2006

All rights reserved. No part of this book may be reproduced, stored in a retrieval system or transmitted in any form by any means, electronic, mechanical, photocopying, recording, scanning or otherwise, except under the terms of the Copyright, Designs and Patents Act 1988 or under the terms of a licence issued by The Copyright Licensing Agency Ltd, 90 Tottenham Court Road, London W1T 4LP UK (www.cla.co.uk), without the written permission of the publisher.

The moral right of the authors has been asserted.

This book sets out to provide accurate information and general advice on the subject matters covered. It is published in good faith, but neither the publisher nor authors can accept liability for loss or expense as a result of relying on particular statements in the book. This book is sold on the clear understanding that the publisher is not involved in providing a professional service. If in doubt about any particular circumstances, readers are advised to seek reliable professional advice before taking any action based upon information provided in this book.

New Venture Publishing Ltd
29 Tivoli Road, Brighton
East Sussex BN1 5BG

E-mail: info@newventurepublishing.co.uk
www.helpinghandbooks.co.uk

ISBN: 0-9552336-1-5
978-0-9552336-1-6

British Library cataloguing-in-publication data
A catalogue record for this book is obtainable from the British Library

Cover design by Mark Tennent
Typeset in Caslon by Mark Tennent, Worthing, West Sussex
Printed and bound by RPM Reprographics Ltd, Chichester, West Sussex

About the authors
Carol Kennedy is a distinguished management author and award-winning business journalist. Formerly executive editor of *Director*, the Institute of Directors' monthly magazine, she is now a regular contributor to the magazine. Her other books include the best-selling *Guide to the Management Gurus* (Random House) and *The Next Big Idea* (Random House).

Peter Bartram is an experienced business writer and journalist who has contributed to a wide range of newspapers and magazines. He edited *Bidding for Business: the Skills Agenda* (Policy Publications) upon which this book is based. His other books include *How to Write the Perfect Press Release* (New Venture Publishing) and *The Information Agenda* (Management Books 2000).

Contents

1	The new competitive landscape	1
2	Making a winning presentation	9
3	Defining product value in customers' terms	15
4	Learning how customer buying centres work	22
5	Building or redesigning a bidding process	28
6	Completing tender documents successfully	33
7	Finding and using competitive intelligence	41
8	Drafting proposals	48
9	Developing key messages about company and products	55
10	Managing the prospect relationship	61
11	Identifying potential new customers	68
12	Developing bid team leadership	74
13	Managing a bid team	81
14	Defining and managing a bid team budget	87
15	Developing bid team communication skills	92
16	Recruiting and training bid team members	97

17	Developing negotiating skills	102
18	Understanding the role of internal stakeholders	109
19	Understanding global bidding trends	114
20	Pitching against international competitors	121
21	Developing and using reference sites	128

Chapter 1

The new competitive landscape

We live in a binary world.

You are either a winner or a loser. More than that, you win big or you lose big. You scoop the pool or you are left with nothing.

An exaggeration? An over-simplification? Yes, to a certain extent. But sometimes it's necessary to exaggerate to make an important point with sufficient power so that the people who need to take notice wake up and take action.

The fact is that competition the world over has become tougher, is becoming tougher and will become tougher in the future. But perhaps the toughness of competition is only part of the issue. After all, winning new business has always been a rough old game. The big difference is that in the bad old days you knew who your competitors were. You faced up to them time and time again in one pitch for new business after another. You learnt about their strengths and weaknesses. Perhaps they also learnt about some of yours, too.

But today it's different. And not just because competitors you've not registered before appear suddenly out of the wide blue yonder. It is a truism to say that we're experiencing the globalisation of business. But that truism masks an important competitive shift.

The fact is that new competitors can now appear from almost any part of the globe. It's true that, in some countries, there are barriers to completely open competition, but they don't undermine the fundamental point that new competitors from growing economies in regions such as the far east, eastern Europe and, increasingly, south America are looking at the world's more developed markets with envious eyes.

And the fact that they often come from low-cost economies with an in-built ability to undercut on price is not the least of their threats. Often, their cultures bring a new freshness, new insights or new technologies to bear which prove even more difficult to counter as competitive challenges. They may invade existing markets, but they may also invent new ones to supplant the old.

But the business that wants to thrive in the binary world can't spend all its time worrying about threats to its existing markets. It has, itself, to seek new horizons. These may be in fresh geographical markets or in new product or service areas, perhaps drawing on existing experience to penetrate an adjacent market sector or using new technologies in an innovative way to become a first-mover in a newly created market of its own.

Whatever its business strategy, it needs to become more skilled at the art of winning new business. The race is, indeed, "not only to the swift" and sometimes companies with excellent products or services lose out to companies with inferior offerings but superior business winning skills. It is no longer enough to trust in that business adage about building a better mousetrap and waiting for the world to beat a path to your door. Somebody with only an adequate mousetrap but excellent sales skills may already have cleaned up the market. In short, it's no longer the case – if it ever was – that superior product plus adequate sales skills beats adequate product plus superior sales skills. Perhaps it might do some of the time. But some of the time is not enough for the big winners in a binary world.

THE NEW COMPETITIVE LANDSCAPE

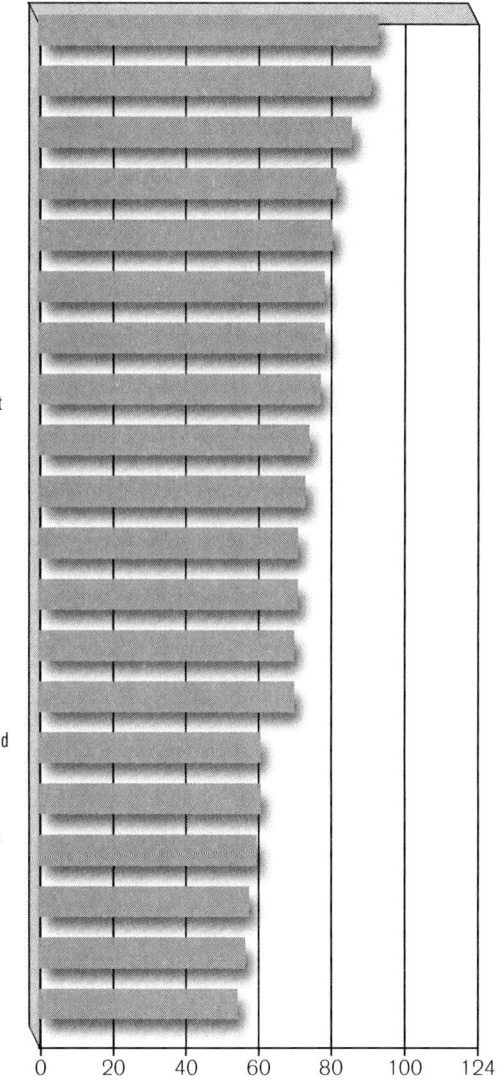

Figure 1. Bidding for business: how much companies want to improve individual skills

1. Making a winning presentation
2. Defining product value in customer's terms
3. Learning how customer buying centres work
4. Building or redesigning a bidding process
5. Completing tender documents successfully
6. Finding and using competitive intelligence
7. Drafting proposals
8. Developing key messages about company & product
9. Managing the prospect relationship
10. Identifying potential new customers
11. Developing bid team leadership
12. Managing a bid team
13. Defining and managing a contract bid budget
14. Developing bid team communication skills
15. Recruiting and training bid team members
16. Developing negotiating skills
17. Understanding the role of internal stakeholders
18. Understanding global bidding trends
19. Pitching against internal competitors
20. Developing and using reference sites

Methodology: 62 companies across a range of business areas were asked whether they were "very interested" (2 points), "quite interested" (1 point) or "not interested" (0 points) in developing their bidding skills. Total mark out of a maximum of 124

What is encouraging is that there are plenty of directors and other senior managers in many management disciplines – not just marketing and sales – who recognise the need to sharpen their company's performance when pitching for new business. This book is based on research with 62 companies in many different industries who habitually find themselves bidding for contracts against well-organised and resourced competitors.

We asked each of the companies whether they were "very interested", "quite interested" or "not interested" in improving each of 20 key bidding skills. When a company was "very interested" in improving a skill, we awarded it two points. We gave one point for "quite interested" and no point for "not interested". Then we added up the scores for each of the 20 skills. The highest mark of 98 (out of a maximum possible of 124) was for "making a winning presentation", while the lowest mark of 60 went to "developing and using reference sites". In between, marks for the remaining 18 skills were tightly bunched as figure one on page 3 shows.

It is not without significance that the most highly rated skills, including "defining product value in customer's terms" and "learning how customer buying centres work", are those which focus most sharply on immediate customer concerns. This suggests that many companies don't feel that they perform well enough at these issues and want to improve.

Conversely, those skills which companies are least interested in improving, including "understanding global bidding trends" and "pitching against internal competitors", are often more theoretical or of specialised interest. The lower points score may reflect the fact that these skills are of practical concern to fewer companies rather than that all the companies are less interested in improving

Figure 2. Bidding for business: how much companies want to raise overall level of skills

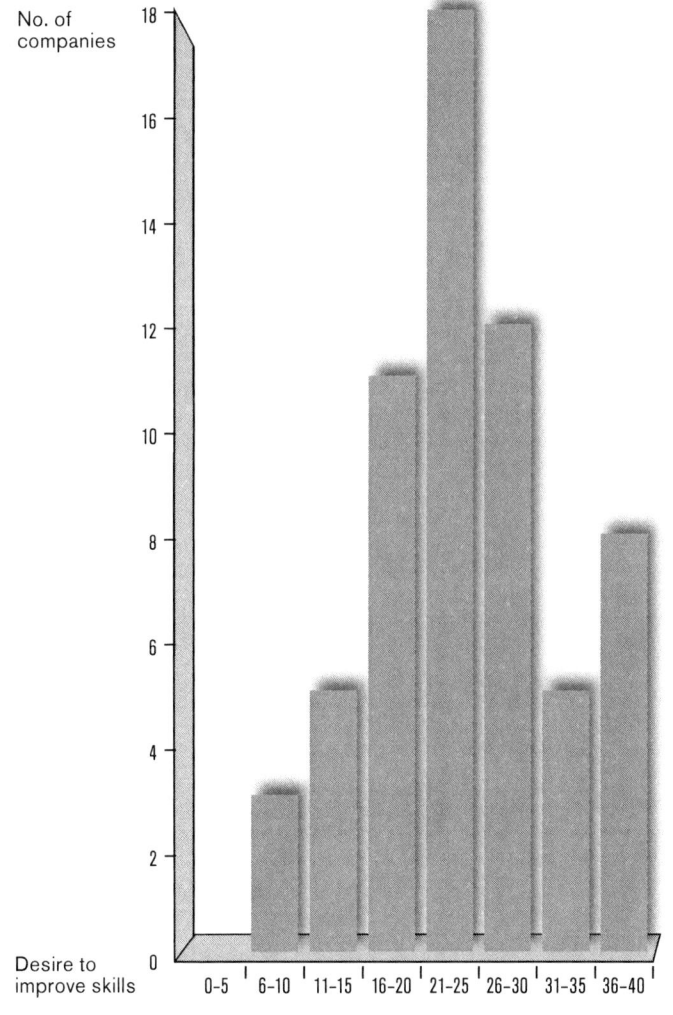

Methodology: each company was marked out of 40 on the basis of how interested it was in improving its skills. This table shows how the 62 companies spread across different bands – the higher the mark, the more interested the company is in skills improvement.

their performance at them. In other words, the fewer companies for whom such skills are important, may still be anxious to raise their game in these areas.

Overall, the picture is one of companies wanting to improve skills across quite a wide canvas. And this is reinforced when we look at how concerned individual companies are in wanting to raise their skills. We calculated this by adding up the total points each company scored against the 20 skills using the same formula, two for "very interested", one for "quite interested" and none for "not interested" (figure two on page 5). Eight of the 62 companies scored between 36 and 40 points (the maximum), displaying a keen desire to improve bidding skills right across the board. A further five scored between 31 and 35 points.

Some of these companies may have a sense of endemic weakness across all or most of their bidding skills, perhaps reflected in a poor win rate when pitching against competitors. But it seemed more likely that most of them were world-class companies with an unquenchable thirst for the management gospel of continuous improvement.

Most of the companies – 44 out of the 62 – bunch towards the centre of figure two with between 16 and 30 points. Again, it can be dangerous to generalise as each company has its own unique agenda, but most of the companies have a clear view of priority areas for improvement while remaining confident about their proficiency at some bidding skills. Just eight companies out of the total show a low interest in improving bidding skills at all – with fewer than 15 points. In fact, three score fewer than 10 points, demonstrating a possibly alarming level of insouciance. It seems likely that the low interest in improving bidding skills in at least some of these companies is not the result of superior world-beating performance, but a consequence of failing to appreciate the standards increasingly required to take on and beat determined competitors.

Information about how much companies want to improve bidding skills may be interesting in a general sense, but the purpose of this book is to provide more than interesting information. Rather, it is to help managers focus on those skills which are most important in their own organisations, then draw up action plans in order to improve them. Because it is a book for managers who already have a keen appreciation of the challenges posed by competitive bidding, we have not gone back to square one on each issue to explain the basics. Rather, we endeavour to focus on those issues which are of greatest concern in a business climate in which global competition is becoming the norm rather than the exception.

Similarly, this is not a book in which grandmothers are invited to suck eggs. The purpose is to help you determine priorities and set agendas, so the text attempts to point to directions and to suggest actions, rather than becoming bogged down in detailed analysis. You may want the more detailed analysis on those skills which are of most importance to your company. To help with that, we have provided a further reading list (under "Bookshelf") for each of the 20 skills. You may also need professional assistance from specialists when you set out to raise your game. We have provided for that by including lists of specialists who may be helpful in each chapter's "Resource Centre", although we should make it clear that we are not specifically recommending any of the organisations listed and you should always check references carefully before engaging the services of specialists.

With 20 skills, your first step is to prioritise – to decide which are most important in your company, which are performed at world-class levels and which need to be improved. Merely focusing on what's important and what's less so can, in itself, be a valuable management exercise in terms of planning for the future and directing resources. It is, after all, not possible to change everything at once and you certainly shouldn't try. The Pareto Law – 20 per cent of the effort delivers 80 per cent of the improvement – is likely to apply as much to bidding skills as to other areas of business.

But building bidding skills is not a one-off exercise. It's a continual task in which you – and your competitors – seek progressively to raise the bar to a point at which only you can clear it. You can be certain that if you succeed in reaching this point, it will be only a matter of time before a competitor is capable of making a similar leap. And so the task of improving must start all over again.

Those companies which win business again and again – and will still be doing so in 10 years' time – are those for whom this process of constant renewal comes naturally. The future's losers will be those who believe that success today guarantees success tomorrow. That is a dangerously corrosive belief because it induces a complacency which eats away slowly at business performance.

Happily, complacency doesn't seem to be a problem for most of the companies we surveyed. Rather, there is a new realism and a determination to build skills to match – and, if possible, exceed – those of competitors. That is where the business of winning those new contracts that are vital to sustain success really starts.

Chapter 2

Making a winning presentation

Your presentation or pitch is the key interface with your prospective customer – the culmination of all your work on winning the bid – and your prime opportunity to influence the customer in your favour. This is where you get to showcase your plus points – your superior product or service, the quality of the team that will be responsible for delivering and backing it up, and your company's reputation in the marketplace. The final pitch can be make-or-break for winning the contract especially when the ultimate choice comes down to two or three closely matched contenders.

In a winning presentation, you establish a real relationship with the people you present to. A winning presentation makes the client feel: these are people we want to do business with. The whites-of-their-eyes factor may make all the difference between choosing one supplier over another.

Key issues

If it is to be a team presentation, select your team members carefully to provide a good mix of talent and individuality, so that each person can contribute something fresh to hold audience interest. The quality of the team, not just the team leader, is often the deciding factor. You may need key people such as your engineering director, IT director or marketing director to explain to the client how they fit into the process and can help achieve the client's needs.

If a team is to give the presentation, rehearse it together so that it runs smoothly without hesitation or confusion over individual roles. The audience will note how the team members work together and respond to each other, how well they are organised.

Check out your prospect's team: how many will be there, what are their roles, what will they expect, how big is the room? This information enables you to tailor your pitch more effectively.

Speak from notes or cue cards, never from a script. The client already has the details of your pitch: you are complementing it, not repeating it. Take key messages from the detailed pitch, write them down and heighten their impact. Each team member should contribute a key message.

> **Case in point**
>
> Presentations need to start with a bang. Take the case of the American management guru who marched on stage to loud applause from 200 business people. Without a word, he set down his briefcase, opened it with a click, pulled out an American football and tossed it into the audience. With this single, unexpected move he had his audience hooked and attentive, thinking: what's this for, what will he do or say next?

Highlight the benefits of each part of your proposal as soon as you can. It's known by some experts as "putting the headline upfront" – people are more interested in the outcome than in the process.

Don't overdo visual aids or have complicated slides that are hard to read. They confuse both audience and speaker. Work out what you want to say, then decide which aids best support it.

Overcome nerves by understanding your material thoroughly. Planning and practice will provide confidence that you can give a competent presentation. The audience will not know how nervous you are under that competent delivery. Breathing exercises help to calm tension and improve tone and resonance. The more presentations you do, the easier it gets.

Don't waffle, keep to the point and don't overrun your speaking time. If you know one of your client's team is the managing director, don't give all your eye contact to him or her – spread your attention around. Don't give the impression that this is a routine presentation: the client must feel everything is tailored to its particular needs. Allow plenty of time for questions and feedback. Questions will tell you if your audience has fully understood the presentation.

Ask yourself what your questions would be if you were on the other side, including those you would least like to hear. Don't be too quick to answer – a pause indicates you are thinking about the question.

Don't get defensive at challenging or unfriendly questions – stay cool and courteous. If a question refers to your company having failed in the past, don't dwell on old problems but move on to explain how much better the company is now. Manipulate questions to your advantage – use even a negative question as a way into a positive point.

Action plan

Conduct a skills audit of staff who make regular pitches for new business. How many have made presentations? How many have been trained in presentation making? Who are your best presenters – watch out for hidden talent?

Establish a properly funded training programme to enhance skills where necessary. Assess whether it can be done in-house or will need professional help from outside.

Draw up a best practice guide for making good presentations and distribute it to all likely team members. Make certain everybody making presentations understands what is expected. Don't forget technical or back-office staff who may occasionally need to take part in a presentation team. They may need some training too.

Bookshelf

Creative Business Presentations: Inventive Ideas for Making an Instant Impact by Eleri Sampson (Kogan Page). First half provides presentation basics. Second half looks at how to use verbal, visual and aural ideas to make your audience sit up and take notice.

Presenting to Win: the Art of Telling Your Story by Jerry Weissman (FT Prentice Hall). Presentation consultant gives his tips on how to dump that Powerpoint presentation and enthrall your audience by telling a compelling story.

Effective Presentation, by Antony Jay, former chairman of training company Video Arts (Institute of Management/Pitman Publishing) Practical step-by-step guide, from planning to giving the presentation. Useful advice on speaking effectively, handling the audience and using visual aids.

The Perfect Presentation, by Andrew Leigh and Michael Maynard (Century). Pocket-sized, quick and easy introduction to the essentials. Its main message: be prepared and be yourself.

How to Be Better at Giving Presentations, by Michael Stevens (Kogan Page, in association with the Industrial Society). Clear and practical guide to knowing the audience, preparing the talk, using aids, rehearsing and preventing last-minute glitches.

Resource Centre

The following provide training in business presentation skills.

Aziz Corporation
No 1, Aziz Court
Parkhill
Winchester
Hampshire SO21 3QX
01962 774766

Bladonmore
10-11 Percy Street
London W1T 1DA
020 7631 1155
www.bladonmore.com

Coulter Ford Associates
Cedarmount House
90a Owlsmoor Road
Owlsmoor, Sandhurst
Berkshire GU47 0SS
Tel: 01252 313674

The Presentation Business
Unit 38
105 London Road
Reading RG1 4QD
0870 751 3971
www.presentationbiz.co.uk

Training Solutions
Greentrees House
Woodside
Grange Road
London N12 8SS
Tel: 020 8446 6005
www.trainingsolutions-int.co.uk

TRT
The Studio
4 Leeds Road
Sheffield S9 3TY
0114 242 4383
www.t-r-t.co.uk

Chapter 3

Defining product value in customer's terms

Your bid has a value to the customer not only in terms of price but also because of the benefits your proposed solution provides. Each aspect of your offer has a specific value which may be high or low depending upon the customer's unique requirements. Understanding the level of value that your customer places on solutions to each need – where the need is most pressing and where it is marginal – is the foundation of a successful bid.

Value innovation – ensuring that the client's most important issues are dealt with effectively – is key here. When it's assessing proposals, the customer may add together individual values of each element of the bid to produce a consolidated value. To win, therefore, your bid has to have a consolidated value higher than those of your competitors.

Key issues

Use market and customer research imaginatively to discover what customers or groups of similar customers really want. Focus especially on what they are likely to need in the future. Use the research to identify new problems likely to be common to groups of companies in a particular market.

In assessing the needs of potential customers, keep two key points in mind. First, don't confine your strategy within your industry's accepted parameters but look for ideas that will give clients quantum leaps in value. Second, focus on new services or products that competitors cannot immediately provide. Benchmarking yourself against competitors, while useful, only yields incremental advantages in the bid.

Do not focus solely on the traditional competitive issues of price and quality but on whether you can provide the customer with additional benefits that may not be present in other bids. Can you give your customer a technical edge or help it capture a more dominant market share? Will your own geographical position – as a local company or a worldwide player – enable the customer to acquire inside knowledge or an entry point into new markets?

Ask yourself whether there are any additional aspects to your bid that the customer won't really value but see only as cost items. Look at whether you can deliver key aspects of the bid at a lower cost. Examine whether you can use different materials or construction methods and still offer similar quality or performance. Involve not only designers, engineers and technical specialists but suppliers and business partners.

To gain a more detailed picture of the issues clients value most highly, examine point-by-point the factors that will most influence the purchase decision. These might include interest rates and the current level of inflation; the laws regulating the industry or commercial environment in which the client operates; government policies and constraints; the climate and geographical location; and the international quality standards commonly applied or demanded by the buyer's own customers.

Remember that complexity and value – the two most influential purchase characteristics – are relative to the buyer. For instance, the purchase of large numbers of cars is of lower complexity and higher value to Hertz than, say, Unilever. This drives home the message that it is the buyer's perceptions of complexity and value that matter and that relatively low complexity or value to the seller can be, for a first-time buyer, difficult and risky. Similarly, the greater the value of the purchase to the size and worth of the buying company, the greater the need for control over its cost.

Finally, remember that innovation does not always mean that you continually have to come up with breakthroughs in new products or services – you can make incremental changes to improve many aspects of your existing portfolio or take other people's ideas a stage further to get the edge. Instil innovation throughout the bid, not just in the technical solution but in the commercial response, the financing and pricing, the presentation of your offer and in the bid management process itself. An imaginative fee or pricing structure that helps the client fit the project into this year's budget could prove as creative a response to his or her needs as an incremental improvement to your product.

Action plan

Use your access to the right competitive intelligence (see chapter seven) to assess which aspects of your bid are likely to be valued most by the client. Extend this not only to the product or service on offer but to the way the bid is financed, managed and structured. In the successful bid by a contract publishing house for a major telecom company's new customer magazine (see case in point, chapter nine), the winning factor was the effort the contract publisher placed on demonstrating its understanding of the telecom supplier's small to medium-sized customers – the key target readership – rather than production quality, an attribute that was matched by the other three competitors.

Use the same technique to assess the impact of the project on the client. Is it a small part of its overall business development strategy, such as the purchasing of regular supplies, or a major diversion from the way it normally does things? Does the client's viability rest on the success of the project? In one company's successful pitch to be one of the key service providers to a leading PC supplier, the

---

Case in point

The importance of value innovation is illustrated by a French hotel and catering giant's strategy. In re-launching its chain of budget hotels, it asked four key questions about customer needs: Which factors our industry takes for granted could be eliminated? Which factors could be reduced below industry standards? Which factors should be raised above industry standards? Which new factors should be created that the industry has never offered? The hotel chain eliminated many standard features not valued highly by budget hotel customers, such as restaurants, bars and 24-hour reception. It invested more in features that customers prized most highly – bed quality and sound proofing. It provided two-star quality on these features at a one-star price. By going beyond the competition, the hotel chain changed the market.

---

approach was dictated by the managing director's assessment that it was no small decision for the PC supplier to change a service provider because its function lay at the heart of the PC supplier's key relationship with its customers. In these circumstances, the PC supplier was looking for a partner not a supplier and the bidding company's pitch stressed the long-term compatibility between the two firms' cultures.

Bookshelf

The International Handbook of Market Research Techniques, editor Robin Birn (Kogan Page). A core text for anybody interested in market research.

Market Research: an Integrated Approach by Dr Alan Wilson (Pearson Education). Official textbook for students of the joint Marketing Research/Chartered Institute of Marketing module on market research.

Market Research, by Paul Hague and Peter Jackson (Kogan Page). An excellent summary of how market research can be linked to business planning, with strong emphasis on assessing the real needs of clients.

Successful Business Strategy, by Len Hardy (Windrush Books). Contains an excellent chapter on "best value" in business, which is closely related to the concept of value innovation. The same section also includes chapters on competitive advantage and market leadership.

Customer Value Management, by Merlin Stone and Harvey Thompson (Policy Publications). A briefing in the *Close to the Customer* series which provides a methodology for helping you to offer customers the kind of benefits they find most valuable.

Resource Centre

Chartered Institute of Marketing
Moor Hall
Cookham
Maidenhead
Berkshire SL6 9QH
Tel: 01628 427500
www.cim.co.uk
The premier professional marketing organisation in the UK

For more information about market research:

Market Research Society
15 Northburgh Street
London EC1V 0JR
020 7490 4911
www.marketresearch.co.uk

British Market Research Association
Devonshire House
60 Goswell Road
London EC1M 7AD
United Kingdom
020 7566 3636
www.bmra.org.uk

Alliance of International Market Research Institutes
26 Granard Avenue
London SW15 5HJ
020 8730 3343
www.aemri.org

European Federation of Associations of Market Research
Organisations
Hoek van Hollandlaan 13
2554 EA Den Haag
The Netherlands
+31-10-28.94.505

Chapter 4

Learning how customer buying centres work

Understanding the customer's buying centre is essential to any successful bid. The buying centre does not just include the members of the purchasing team but anyone, internal or external, who influences the decision. Each company has its own model for taking major purchasing decisions, even if it hasn't formally designed that model or acknowledged its existence. Pinpointing the decision factors that differ from those in other companies is hard from the outside – but success in this helps to determine who wins and who loses.

Bidders need to determine the factors which influence the purchasing decision – the influence and input of individuals on the purchasing team and those outside the team who have an interest in the outcome. They must understand the ways in which the client's view of the factors in the purchase decision might be affected by any communications campaign that the bidder generates.

Key issues

Learn more about how purchasing operates in the industries you serve. Speak to purchasing professionals, study purchasing literature. Look especially at how purchasing professionals take decisions and at the roles played by other managers in purchasing decisions.

Pinpoint factors most likely to influence the purchase decision. These might be economic, legal, political, technological, social or cultural. In some countries, for example, government policies, tariffs and constraints on military spending might be part of the equation. In others, a strong ethic of technology transfer might mean that the product's capacity for easy transfer to local communities could take precedence over state-of-the-art excellence.

Assess the likely impact of the complexity of the product or service on the purchase decision. The more technically complex a product, the more people and departments will be involved. Technically sophisticated and complex purchases are also more likely to be more expensive and thus involve more senior levels of management.

Case in point

A medical equipment company exports to Asian countries where customer buying centres may have a wide range of influencers. When selling in China, it discovered that people who would subsequently operate the equipment were key influencers. Providing educational workshops and training materials proved to be a key factor. This enabled the equipment operators to pass on knowledge to front-line medical staff in hospitals. Addressing the needs of the influencers was key to winning the business.

Assess the value of the purchase in relation to the size and worth of the buyer. The greater the value, the greater the need for control over its cost and the more likely that membership of the buying centre will be dispersed throughout the organisation.

Find out who identified the need for the purchase in the first place, and whether the circumstances that led to the decision were expected or unexpected. This helps you understand why the company is making the purchase.

Keep track of people changes in the client's buying centre, which may alter at each "buy stage" of the purchase. In the early stage, the buying centre will be dominated by technical experts. During the search for suppliers, the purchasing department is dominant and during evaluation the internal client's influence is king.

Find people in the client organisation with influence and power you can enlist to your side. You need someone to spotlight your motives, stress the values that your involvement brings and champion the benefits of your proposal in the right places. Sometimes such people may be found within the purchasing team itself. In other cases, they may be recruited from the wider range of stakeholders in the customer's buying centre (see chapter 18).

A well-targeted communications campaign is vital if newcomers encountering a buying centre for the first time are to get on a short-list. Experience and academic research show that suppliers who have worked with the purchaser before are favoured over an unknown quantity.

Time your campaign to occur at the point when the buyer moves from defining the need to determining the ideal characteristics of the product. If an unknown bidder waits until the point where the buyer is drawing up a short-list before establishing contact, it may be too late.

Follow up advertising with formal contact through a sales campaign to establish a personal relationship with the potential buyer. The five priorities of any sales campaign should be to establish personal credibility; undertake market research that will provide inside information for any presentation; influence the design specification in favour of the bidder; establish the firm's credibility; and establish the best means of communication.

Action plan

If you have bid for contracts with the customer before, conduct an audit of the information you already have about its likely buying centre and update information realistically. Are you bidding for a contract that will have a similar technical specification and, as a consequence, will the same departments and technical expertise be represented on the team? Does the company have a centralised purchasing function that remains unchanged from bid to bid or does the whole make-up of the buying centre change according to the specific contract? How long since you last bid for a contract with the company? What economic, legal, political or technological changes have occurred since then which may change how the company considers the bid? Don't forget to consider factors such as a merger or acquisition, a change in government or a change in regulations.

Now concentrate on key individuals. How many of the same individuals still work for the customer and/or are likely to remain members of the purchasing team? Of the new members, how many are either likely to be well-disposed to your bid or are sufficiently well-briefed about your firm to have a proper understanding of your strengths? How many insiders in either the purchasing team or the overall customer buying centre are likely to be fighting for your pitch? What existing contacts between your firm and the customer can be used to change this situation in your favour?

If you have not previously pitched to this organisation before, what inside information can you gain that will give you a comprehensive picture of the make-up of its buying centre? Have any senior managers inside your firm had dealings with the prospective customer earlier in their careers? Can you co-opt onto the bid team someone who has the right inside knowledge (see chapter 16)? If not, should you be thinking of collaborating in a joint bid with a local supplier?

Plan your communications campaign carefully. Launch any advertising campaign early in the process and target it at the people responsible for transforming the need into a formal specification. Integrate any follow-up sales campaign with the key messages contained in the advertising, but shift the emphasis from establishing the corporate credibility of the firm to the personal credibility of key members of both the bid team and the project team responsible for implementing the contract. Remember that if you leave everything to the point where the prospective client is drawing up the short-list, it will be too late.

Bookshelf

Crossing the Chasm, by Geoffrey A Moore (Capstone Publications). Shows how to adjust market communications strategies for technological products to the changing needs of prospective customers.

The Customer Driven Organisation, by Richard C Whiteley (Century). A little hard-sell on the methods used by the author's consultancy, The Forum Corporation, but it contains a good chapter on creating a customer-driven vision.

Winning New Business…the Critical Success Factors, by Carol Kennedy and Matthew O'Connor (Policy Publications). Contains a detailed chapter on how buyers make decisions.

Developing Strategic Customers & Key Accounts…the Critical Success Factors by John Hurcomb (Policy Publications). Contains key information about building strategic relationships with key customers at every level. Explores what the most successful companies do more effectively.

Targeting High-Value Customers by Merlin Stone et al, (Policy Publications). A briefing in the *Close to the Customer* series, it uses the airlines as a paradigm to show how important it is to understand more about valuable customers.

RESOURCE CENTRE

To look at purchasing from the "other side of the fence", gather information from purchasing professionals:

Chartered Institute of Purchasing and Supply
Easton House
Easton-in-the-Hill
Stamford
Lincolnshire PE9 3NZ
01780 756777
www.cips.org
Leading organisation for UK purchasing professionals

European Institute of Purchasing Management
International Business Park
French Geneva Campus
74166 Archamps
France
+33 4 50 31 56 78
www.eipm.org
Important European centre for studying purchasing issues

Chapter 5

Building or redesigning a bidding process

The bid process is the heart of your strategy. All bid processes go through six major phases and many minor ones, according to professional bid manager Neil Tweedley: identifying a prospect; developing the opportunity; preparing a plan and recruiting the bid team; submitting the bid proposal; evaluating the result and, if successful, carrying out the project. Setting up an organised framework for the bidding process helps to marshal all the information inputs, to see the bid from both supplier's and buyer's perspective, and to cope with the time and resource pressures that often force a bidder into cutting corners or making snap decisions.

Successful bidders start early and work within a structured bidding process that incorporates their own proven best practices. The structure should also enhance your chances of winning future bids by maintaining a good management information system at each stage of the bid and providing feedback, reinforcing the successful elements and removing those that failed. "Effective bid management systems require constant attention," says Tweedley.

Key issues

Decide what your bid process is trying to achieve, and analyse how the existing system works. Does it need a fundamental redesign or a major rethink? How does your bid process compare with what you know of your most successful competitors?

Key issues to look for in improving the existing system are:

inherent delays, redundant or duplicated processes, critical dependencies on a particular IT system or personnel, the flow of information and decision-making. Aim for a simplified, cost-effective process. Don't just look at doing the same things better but at doing things in better ways. Document your new bidding process thoroughly so that everyone knows how it works.

Organise the bidding process around your key differentiator against your competitors – what your client is willing to pay more for. Make sure this is represented in the composition of your bidding team.

Design the bidding process so that the bid can withstand problems – for example, if a key person is sick, someone else can run with it. This means keeping an accurate record of progress at all times.

Build quality into all aspects of your bidding process, such as BS5750/ISO9000 standards. Some clients will insist on

---

Case in point

An engineering company with businesses in defence and aerospace, the nuclear industry and bulk material handling, has implemented a new "business generation" process. It helps the company identify and pursue bid opportunities, put in bids and convert the bids to orders. Explains the company's business improvement process project manager: "At one time, we had six different divisions, each of which identified its own opportunities. It could mean different divisions were competing for the same work." The new process rationalises the company's bidding approach and is leading to more wins.

compliance. Make sure the bid process is recorded and monitored through an effective bid information system integrated with your company's management information network. This should provide status reports, financial forecasts, business benefits, documentation control.

Retain all the core data in preparing the proposal for at least one year to enable reworking, if necessary, and implementation of the contract. Ensure that the bidding process provides opportunities for learning and continuous improvement.

Action plan

After analysing your current bid process, identify its best practice elements and incorporate them into a structured framework which can form the basis for future winning bids and help maximise the skills and human resources available. The redesigned, standardised bid process should cover everything from identifying a bidding opportunity to the contract decision.

Make sure you have all the management information you need to monitor progress and to keep the bidding process running smoothly. Integrate the bidding process with other information sources wherever necessary.

Set up a checklist to keep track of such objectives as quantifying risk, bid registration systems and BS5750/ISO9000 document control. Provide common sources of regularly used information to bid teams.

Decide whether to use a specialist IT contract bidding system. If so explore the various products offered by suppliers. Decide whether to use a packaged approach or build a bespoke system using one of the generic software suppliers.

Build in an effective debriefing system after the success or failure of each bid to weed out unsuccessful elements of the bidding process and strengthen those that worked. Inculcate a learning culture in everybody involved with winning bids.

Bookshelf

Winning the Bid: a Manager's Guide to Competitive Bidding, by Neil Tweedley (FT/Pitman Publishing). Tweedley is a professional bid manager and chartered engineer with a background in telecoms and IT systems where he manages bid opportunities for companies. His book is an excellent single-volume guide to competitive bidding and chapter two contains practical tips on structuring a bid.

Business Process Re-engineering: Myth and Reality by Colin Coulson-Thomas (editor) (Kogan Page). Collection of studies that look at the practical implications of redesigning bidding processes.

Resource Centre

Consultants:

Adaptation
Mill Reach
Mill Lane
Water Newton
Cambridgeshire PE8 6LY
01733 361149
Consultancy organisation of Professor Colin Coulson-Thomas, a leading specialist in business process management.

Insight
Morland Hall
Morland
Cumbria CA10 3BB
01931 714714
www.insight-organisation.com
Insight founder and managing director Neil Tweedley is the auther of *Winning the Bid* (Financial Times), the current standard business textbook.

Sales process management software supplier:

Cincom Systems (UK)
1 Grenfell Road
Maidenhead
Berkshire SL6 1HN
01628 542300
Product: Sales Process Automation
www.cincom.com

Chapter 6

Completing tender documents successfully

For certain bids – most commonly in the public sector and with global development agencies – detailed tender documents drawn up by the client determine which contenders are short-listed. Compliance with the specification outlined in the tender documentation is strictly enforced and if your interpretation of what is required is wrong, it may lose you the contract.

Check the terms carefully to see what special conditions apply. Evaluate the strictures applying to price. Clarify anything that may seem ambiguous in the invitation to tender. Start the work early – completing tenders often takes longer than you think.

Key issues

Bids for formal tenders of this kind are generally published in advance to allow bidders time to assess the feasibility of the project and plan their strategy. It may be worthwhile subscribing to publications where notices are placed – for example, *Development Business* (see sources of help on page 40) in the case of the United Nations – or to another service that alerts you to forthcoming tenders.

Compliance with bidding rules is vital. Your bid can and will be eliminated from the assessment if you contravene any of them. Even seemingly trivial rules regarding the completion and delivery of tender documents must be followed. If a competitor points out that you have contravened the packaging or labelling rules, the agency may be duty bound to uphold his complaint, wasting months of diligent effort.

For this reason, seek expert advice where it is offered. In many aid-funded bids, for example, consultants are often used to supplement local technical expertise, independently assessing the bids received. Although tender documents are drawn up in the country carrying out the project, it is with the assistance of the lending agency and consultant. You should establish contact with the consultant, if allowed, and seek early clarification about any aspect of the documentation on which you are unclear.

Similarly, avoid submitting a conditional response with reservations or caveats because you have not obtained sufficient information. This can result in your proposal being viewed less favourably than others. You may be able to negotiate on critical issues later.

In any aid-funded bid, price is a critical factor. The way in which the tender documentation reflects a right or wrong interpretation of the bid's budgetary considerations will often decide which firms are short-listed. Prices usually have to be submitted according to a fixed schedule and it is important not to omit any specified cost item, even if you do not believe it will be used in the general assessment. You may not be able to apply the degree of financial innovation that you can in other bid situations, so good spreadsheet calculations are especially important.

If you cannot massage your prices to fit the required specification, always stress the economic advantages of your fee or pricing structure. Even if these factors are not taken into consideration in the main assessment, they could become the deciding factor between two finely balanced bids.

Tender documentation is equally important in bids for

European Union projects. Recent directives require a more open approach, making this market sector more accessible to small and medium-sized companies. Ironically, this has resulted in stricter enforcement of tender regulations to prevent abuse of the rules. As in bids for aid-funded projects, advice from specialist consultants or EU officials should always be sought if you need to clarify requirements.

The three most important factors in EU bids are official notification, notice periods and the use of international quality standards. As in aid-funded bids, all bids are published, in this case in the *Official Journal Supplement* or its electronic equivalent, *Tenders Electronic Daily*, up to six months ahead. Open tenders have to allow 52 days from the date of invitation to bid notice until the closing date for receipt of bids. Once invited to bid, you are given at least 40 days to submit your bid – although some accelerated bids operate to a much tighter timetable. Compliance with international quality standards, most commonly ISO9000, EN2900 or BS5750, is now almost always required, except where no standard exists or where the project is breaking new ground.

The tender documentation should reflect the criteria most likely to be uppermost in the purchasing agency's decision-making procedures. Price is obviously an important starting point. The selectors are bound to consider the lowest or most advantageously priced bid – but they can take other pricing factors into account, including technical innovation and originality and a track record of exceptional performance.

Expect also to be rigorously checked out for proof of technical competence, sound finances and general good standing. The burden of proof of probity, sometimes to the point of bureaucratic excess, has been pushed very high by regulations designed to demonstrate that the process is transparent and robust in the case of a challenge in court.

> **Case in point**
>
> World aid-funded bids, offered by agencies such as the World Bank Group, the European Bank for Reconstruction and Development and the African Development Bank, are a lucrative source of revenue. But knowing your way around is critical as inexperienced or ill-prepared bidders can become lost in the tender bureaucracy. To be successful, bidders need to place emphasis in tender documents on what the client will get from the bid – such as products and services not available locally, supporting infrastructure to enable the region to develop culturally, or to transfer knowledge and technology. Each lending agency operates its own procedures for tendering and selection, but in nearly every case the selection of the winning bidder is determined by the borrower rather than lender of funds.

The complexity of public sector tendering, if anything, increases as you pitch for contracts closer to home. Compulsory tendering and market testing in the UK present many opportunities for private bidders. But there are still many unresolved issues in the tendering processes and these apply not only to existing aspects of local government, such as refuse collection and catering, but the more sophisticated services now being outplaced such as housing, library services, legal, financial and personnel services and information technology.

Two issues which will have to be addressed or considered in relevant tender documentation are the ambiguities of market testing and the transfer of undertakings. The restrictions placed on external bidders by market testing regulations often make it very hard for them to deploy the flexibility that otherwise might give them a competitive edge. Government departments tend to over-specify the requirements or oblige the contractor to carry out the operations of the department by retaining the existing set-up. Not surprisingly, the majority of these contracts are still awarded to internal bidders. Similarly, the statutory duties imposed on employers to consult with employees and take into account all reasonable concerns when contracting out services have made it very hard for external bidders to exercise their commercial flexibility.

Action plan

Set up a monitoring service that can canvass the publications announcing formal tenders and provide your firm with as much time as possible to prepare the tender documentation. In the case of aid-funded projects and EU contracts, this might be six months or more.

Establish a network of specialist consultants and expert advisers who can help clarify the specifications of the contract and how they should be interpreted and reflected in the tender documentation.

Develop the appropriate spreadsheet technology to enable you to massage your cost estimates so as to meet the specific price criteria used by the purchasers and try to build in long-term economic advantages that may give you the edge over other bidders.

In any capability statements (see chapter eight), emphasise your technical competence to undertake the task and provide evidence of your general good standing. More depends on these factors in a formal tender than in other types of bid. If you are tendering for public sector and EU funded projects on a regular basis, obtain common quality standards like ISO9000 or BS5750.

Bookshelf

The Art of Tendering by P D V Marsh (Gower Technical Press). Comprehensive overview of all issues to do with tendering with plenty of practical advice.

Understanding Tendering and Estimating by A A Kwakye (Ashgate Publishing). Hard-to-find manual which looks at all the basics of tendering and estimating.

The European Union: a Guide through the EC/EU Maze, by Alex Roney and Stanley Budd (Institute of Directors). Although this is a general primer which covers all aspects of the European Union, the chapters on regional funding and the way the EU works, contain much background information for potential bidders for EU contracts.

Managing in the New Local Government, by Paul Joyce, Paul Corrigan and Mike Hayes (Kogan Page). Aimed specifically at professional local government managers, but the chapter on the relationship between managers and service providers provides many insights for the external public sector bidder.

Winning the Bid, by Neil Tweedley (FT/Pitman). Excellent chapter on public sector bidding that includes a detailed consideration of tender documentation.

Resource Centre

European Commission
8 Storey's Gate
London SW1P 3AT
020 7973 1992
www.cec.org.uk

Tenders Electronic Daily (TED)
http://ted.publications.eu.int/official/

European Bank for Reconstruction and Development
1 Exchange Square
London EC2A 2JN
020 7338 6000
www.ebrd.org

Local Government Information Unit
22 Upper Woburn Place
London WC1H 0TB
020 7554 2801
www.lgiu.gov.uk

Local Government Association
Local Government House
Smith Square
London SW1P 3HZ
020 7664 3131
www.lga.gov.uk

British Standards Institution
389 Chiswick High Road
London W4 4AL
020 8996 9000
www.bsi-global.com

United Nations Development Business
+1 212 963 1516
www.devbusiness.com

Chapter 7

Finding and using competitive intelligence

Understanding your markets, customers and competitors is the essential first step to handling bids effectively. This is especially important as the shape of markets is changing more rapidly than ever before and competitors can emerge from unexpected places. The best competitive intelligence operations ally information collection to insightful analysis.

Define what information is key to success in your market. Collect information regularly from different sources and validate its reliability. Look ahead, imagine the future as it might be and what that could mean for your company. Watch your "blind side" for unexpected competitors.

Key issues

Build your information base in a structured way, start early and keep it updated. Make competitive intelligence a recognised function in your company. Train staff in its skills. Carry out intelligence gathering in a systematic way. Prioritise by collecting information that is most useful for decision-making.

Don't ignore the analysis part of competitive intelligence. Raw information may not mean much – but it may contain valuable insights in the hands of skilled analysts.

When it comes to competitors, use SWOT analysis for each competitor profile. Include areas such as technical capability, portfolio range, history of dealings with client and client's likely view of the competitor's product or service and delivery record. This will also give you a better perspective on your own strengths and weaknesses and highlight areas on which you need to focus.

Work out from these profiles how each competitor is likely to respond to the bid, and to his competitors including you. According to one analysis, the approaches could be passive, attacking or defensive. You will need to deal with each approach in a different way.

> **Case in point**
>
> Not long ago, few banks expected supermarkets to be competitors in financial services. Few oil companies expected supermarkets to compete for petrol sales. Few supermarkets expected petrol station chains to hit back and compete on grocery sales. Technology changes markets, too. The Internet is generating more book sales – threatening established book shops. And these kind of mould-breaking changes are everywhere.

The chief secondary sources of competitor intelligence are company reports, bank and consultancy reports, newspapers, trade papers, brochures, online databases and the Internet. The most valuable information usually comes from direct sources, from the bidding process and dealings with the client, from contacts with companies and individuals familiar with the competitor, and from your own in-company knowledge of the market. It has been calculated that up to 70 per cent of the information a company will ever need lies in the heads of its own staff. It is always advisable to validate information through an independent source.

Pull together information from your internal sources, including: the marketing department, PR and press function, legal office, sales department and R&D. Make sure that key managers within each function are aware of the importance that their information will have in any major bid.

Don't forget internal literature produced by prospective customers. This includes not only the annual report but house literature aimed at the firm's stakeholder community. Don't overlook any professional or trade literature that your clients subscribe to on a regular basis.

Action plan

Set up a "source directory" listing where information you need is to be found – through publications, people, reports and databases.

Categorise sources of information under headings that will be relevant to the bid team, the project team and marketing and sales staff responsible for following up new leads.

Filter information to save only that which is relevant to the bid in hand. Rate each piece of information for its importance to the bid. Check and review regularly.

Encourage key staff not only to draw on the data but to add to it. Contributions should also be sought – and made easy to provide – from any front-line manager or professional who may have access to valuable market intelligence. Some companies link the contribution of valuable competitive intelligence to bonuses or incentive schemes.

Once you have a database of customers up and running, keep it up to date and use it. Having detailed knowledge about your own customers itself provides competitive edge.

Don't neglect the analysis part of competitive intelligence. Collecting information for its own sake is of no particular value unless that information is used to produce new insights and inform better decisions. Competitive intelligence should help the company to understand its customers, competitors and markets better.

BOOKSHELF

Competitive Intelligence by J Underwood (Capstone Express Exec). A quick guide to the essentials of competitive intelligence for anybody who has not come across the topic before.

Strategic and Competitive Analysis: Methods and Techniques for Analysing Business by Craig S Fleischer and Babette Bensoussan (Prentice Hall). For the more advanced users, this is a comprehensive look at the techniques used for analysing business and competitive data.

Online Competitive Intelligence: Increase Your Profits Using Cyber-Intelligence by Helen P Burwell, Carl R Ernst (editor) and Michael Sankey (editor) (National Book Network). Competitive intelligence meets cyberspace. Plenty of useful tips on how to use the wealth of materials on the Internet to build effective competitive intelligence.

The Intelligence Edge, by George Friedman, Meredith Friedman, Colin Chapman and John S Baker, Jr (Century). This can be particularly recommended for its state-of-the-art techniques.

Competitive Intelligence by Larry Kahaner (Simon and Schuster). A clear and entertaining how-to primer that shows how to get into the minds and decision-making processes of competitors' senior executives.

Guide to Analysing Companies, by Bob Vause (Economist Books). This covers published reports, balance sheets, income statements, stock market performance, measurement of profitability, liquidity, capital management and strategy – all valuable grist to a prospective bidder.

The Society of Competitive Intelligence Professionals' website – www.scip.org – contains an extensive reading list on the subject.

Resource Centre

Organisations

Society of Competitive Intelligence Professionals
1700 Diagonal Road
Suite 600
Alexandria
Virginia 22314
United States
+1 703 739 0696
Leading global organisation for CI professionals

Consultants

Each has special skills in competitive intelligence

4-consulting
2-8 Miller Crescent
10 Somerset Place
Edinburgh EH10 5HW
0131 447 4546
www.4-consulting.co.uk

Advanced Business Facilities
The Crest
Droxford
Hampshire SO32 3QL
07714 325657
www.abfl.co.uk

Business Data Consulting
Business Centre
5 Blackhorse Lane
London E17 6DS
020 8279 5333
www.bdc-group.co.uk

EMP Intelligence Service
Springfield House
The Avenue
Dallington
Northampton NN5 7AJ
01604 755005
www.emp-is.com

Juniper Consultancy Services
Sheppards Mill
South Street
Uley
Gloucestershire GL11 5SP
01453 860750
www.juniper.co.uk

Wendy Warr & Associates
6 Berwick Court
Holmes Chapel
Cheshire
01477 533837
www.warr.com

Chapter 8

Drafting proposals

The proposal is the first tangible evidence that the customer will see of your ability to fulfil the contract. It is the main chance to get your ideas, your analysis of the situation and your solution across in sufficient detail to prompt the client to take you seriously as a contender.

Match the length and detail of the proposal to the formality of the bid. Get your distinctive analysis of the customer's situation across in a way that convinces it that you really understand what it wants. Start to shape the customer's thinking about its problem in a way that makes your solution seem the appropriate answer.

Key issues

The way you structure your proposal is very important. An informal proposal in a formal bid may make you seem too lightweight or insignificant. Similarly a very formal response to an informal bid will make you seem stuffy or inflexible.

As a general rule, an informal bid will only require a two to five page letter which includes the proposed fee and timescale for the project. This should be supported by a capability statement which highlights the firm's core expertise and recent success stories and a brochure or similar presentation materials which reinforces the credibility of the firm and answers basic questions – such as how long you have been trading, how many staff, what location, what facilities, and so on.

More formal bids generally entail drawing up a "sealed bid" with an estimated price rather than a contractual offer. This should be more detailed and targeted at a variety of key stakeholders in the client firm (see chapter 18), both on and off the purchase team.

The winning purpose of the proposal should be to demonstrate your understanding of the client's needs. It should reflect the importance of the contract to the client, an understanding of the client's own customers and stakeholders and the regulatory and political context governing the contract. A contract publisher's successful bid to publish a telecom provider's new customer magazine (see case in point in chapter nine) was based on its understanding of the small and medium-sized enterprises targeted by the magazine.

The proposal should also establish the right communication channels with the client, setting out clearly who is the main point of contact and a method of operating for day to day liaison. The proposal from the contract publisher to the telecom provider (see above) suggested that after the pitch there should be a further meeting at the publisher's office to allow the telecom provider's key personnel to see the operation at first hand. Although this was also adopted in the case of other competitors, the contract publisher knew that a face-to-face meeting with members of the proposed editorial team would favour them, especially since all could demonstrate first-hand expertise based on many years' experience of business magazine publishing.

Because the written proposal is so central to any bid's success, overall responsibility for planning, preparing and managing its production should be given to the bid manager (see chapter 16). If a separate project manager – who will lead the implementation team if the bid is successful – has been appointed prior to the bid, then the bid manager should work with him or her in drawing up key aspects of the documentation, such as the capability statement and the implementation plan.

Delivery of the proposal should be timely. If you miss the deadline, your bid may not be accepted, but bids submitted too early have been known to disappear. Always get a receipt for the proposal. In addition, leave enough time for the formal text to be approved – you may need to go through various levels of authority, and authorisation on large bids invariably takes longer than expected.

> **Case in point**
>
> Irish bid expert Deiric McCann recommends that every proposal should be subjected to an eight point inspection check before it's issued: (1) accurate definition of the client requirement, (2) match of the proposed solution to the client requirement, (3) identification and communication of key benefits of the proposed solution, (4) accurate and effective presentation of costs, (5) completeness of "proof" material in the appendices, (6) effectiveness of the executive summary, (7) good English use, and (8) good presentation style.

Action plan

Ensure that lines of accountability are straightened out well before the bid. Decide who is to have responsibility for drawing up the key proposals – the manager running the bid or the manager who will run the project if the bid is successful. Determine which senior manager or managers will be responsible for approving the offer and the text of the proposal before it is submitted.

Certain documents that traditionally accompany proposals – capability statements and brochures – can and should be prepared in advance, enabling bid managers to respond quickly to unexpected offers. However, these should be kept regularly updated and, where possible, tailored to meet the specific requirements of the tender.

Producing a large bid document is a significant publication exercise. The bid manager should plan printing well ahead of time and order in advance the binders, paper and consumables needed to complete the printing.

Bookshelf

Persuasive Business Proposals by Tom Sant (Amacom). The main point about this book is how to make customer proposals more customer centred.

Writing Winning Business Proposals: Your Guide to Landing the Client; Making the Sale; Persuading the Boss by Richard C Freed, Sherrin Freed and Joe Romaro (McGraw-Hill Education). Focuses on how to think strategically about writing a proposal and includes useful worksheets.

Winning Business Proposals by Deiric McCann (Oak Tree Press). A comprehensive view of writing proposals with plenty of helpful advice and techniques to use.

How to Be Better at Writing Reports and Proposals, by Patrick Forsyth (Kogan Page). Although this is aimed more at managers who need to impress or convince their internal colleagues, much of the basic good practice is also relevant to the first-time bid manager.

How to Write Winning Proposals for Your Company or Client edited by Ron Tepper (John Wiley & Sons). Collection of essays from US specialists giving an American view of proposal writing with some useful insights for European proposal writers – especially those tackling the US market.

Proposals, Pitches and Beauty Parades: Winning New Business in the '90s by John de Forte and Guy Jones (FT/Pitman) British view of the topics by two authors with first-hand experience of their subject.

Sources of help

UK consultants

Insight
Morland Hall
Morland
Cumbria CA10 3BB
01931 714714
www.insight-organisation.com

US consultants

Web sites with interesting information about proposal writing

The Proposal Group of Len Duffy and Associates
www.lenduffy.com

Shipley Associates
www.shipleywins.com

Proposal writing training courses:

Calyx Communications
PO Box 423
Farnham
Surrey GU9 8UU
01252 725950
www.calyxcomms.co.uk

Emphasis Training
9-12 Middle Street
Brighton BN1 1AL
01273 732888
www.emphasis-training.co.uk

Hawksmere
4th Floor
North West Wing
Bush House
Aldwych
London WC2B 4PJ
020 7632 2300
www.hawksmere.co.uk

LMA Sales Training and Consultancy Services
6 Kensington Silver Wharf
Sovereign Harbour
Eastbourne BN23 5NN
01323 471730
www.lmonk.dircon.co.uk

Chapter 9

Developing key messages about company and product

Understanding and influencing the customer is the key to communicating with it on the same wavelength. Tailoring your key messages to each part of the customer's purchasing strategy – taking into account the level of prior knowledge and credibility of your firm in the customer's eyes – may determine whether you reach that all-important short-list. Successfully distinguishing yourself from your competitors in a second wave of messages moves your company towards the top of the list.

Understanding your own strengths and weaknesses and the needs of the client is an obvious first step in getting onto the short-list. But the winning strategies are those that also understand and anticipate the messages that are likely to be developed by competitors. The aim of the strategy is not to seem as good as the competition in the eyes of the client – but better.

Key issues

The key role of the messages in early communications channels, like advertising and PR promotion, should not be to persuade the purchaser to buy – this is premature – but to persuade potential customers to invite a bid. Bringing the bidder to the attention of the buyer and establishing the firm's track record and credibility should be the main focus.

Once the firm has been invited to bid and the process moves to the tender document, the emphasis of the message shifts. In the documentation, you should focus on your understanding of the client's needs, as gained from any pre-tender client briefings and, equally important, from market knowledge or inside information about internal stakeholder needs (see chapter 18). These should then be matched to your own firm's strengths.

> **Case in point**
>
> When a contract publishing house bid to produce a new customer magazine for a major telecoms provider, it developed strong messages. The first was an understanding of the telecom provider's market needs, which the contract publisher communicated in its proposal and at meetings. The second was its size, reputation and track record. But the contract publisher recognised that the other four companies on the pitch list could boast similar attributes. Pricing was not an issue since the client had a set budget and could choose freely on other criteria. Once the quality of the tender document had placed the contract publisher on the short-list, it focused on value-added factors. Critically, it stressed the quality of the editorial and advertising team, emphasising its generous staffing levels – a factor not stressed by other short-listed firms. The contract publisher also focused on its team's experience and knowledge of the target readership. This placed it in an unassailable position.

Once on the short-list and during a bid presentation and any preparatory or follow-up meetings, focus on establishing the superiority of your products and services over those of your competitors. This should include any "value-added" advantage such as your ability to offer ancillary services and support. The most successful companies are three times more likely to be successful in bids in these key areas (see *Winning New Business...the Critical Success Factors* under Bookshelf on page 59). Messages at this stage should also emphasise the personal credibility of the members of the project team who will undertake the work.

Don't forget the importance of messages aimed at stakeholders who are not represented on the purchase team but who influence the final decision. The ability to quote satisfied customers or reference sites greatly increases the credibility of a bid. In a computer service company's bid to a major PC manufacturer (see case in point in chapter 21 on page 131), the PC manufacturer's ability to reference the computer service company's infrastructure, quality of service and European capability was a key factor. The most important reference is clearly a stream of satisfied customers, but in early stages of the bid, at a time when the capabilities of the bidder may be unknown or unclear to the purchase team, the imaginative use of websites, particularly those with interactive capabilities, is now well established as an effective tool.

"Value" and "security" are key common factors in buyers' criteria and the importance of one over the other varies according to the exact nature of the bid. With routine orders, the main criteria are reliability in delivery and price as well as the ability to meet varying levels of demand. In "procedural problem products" – where performance is predictable but tailoring is necessary – the quality of the technical service and the ability of the supplier to retrain staff to deliver the necessary back-up needs to be emphasised more strongly.

Action plan

Start with some very basic questions. Why is the customer inviting bids at this time? Where does it want to be in the next three to five years and what can your company contribute to its ambitions? What risks are involved in the bid and how can you minimise them? What bottom line requirements are likely to be demanded from all bidders? What are the likely concerns of individual members of the team and the likely influence of external stakeholders such as end-users and senior managers (see chapter 18)?

Next match these against your own firm's capabilities and reputation. Can you provide a perfect solution to all the customer's requirements or do you have to shift its thinking in order to bring it round to considering your firm? Is your firm's reputation in the field sufficiently high for it to be automatically "front of mind" in the case of key members of the purchasing team? Or does its credibility or visibility need to be raised? Who are you likely to be up against? How does your scorecard look compared to their's and what messages are most likely to counteract their strengths?

When assessing these issues, look at the context and nature of the bid. Are you engaged in a bid for a routine order where your track record of reliability, delivery and product quality is at stake? Are you pitching for a high value-added service or product where the credibility of key members of the project team is likely to be the deciding factor?

Now think about the stakeholders. Do the messages aimed at them need to be different from the ones aimed at the purchasing team? Are there any stakeholders likely to be hostile to your bid who need to be singled out for reassurance? Remember that the more focused the message and the more targeted the audience, the more effective the message is likely to be.

Bookshelf

Don't Compete...Till the Field, by Louis Patler (Capstone). More inspirational than how-to, this book looks at how top companies like Fiat, Cadbury-Schweppes and Daimler have repositioned themselves or become market leaders by redefining the market.

Even More Offensive Marketing, by Hugh Davidson (Penguin Books). Davidson is a popular writer in this field, drawing on frontline experience in Procter & Gamble and United Biscuits. There is a good chapter on communications which covers probing analyses of client needs and risk-taking communications campaigns.

Making Sense of Competition Policy, by Frank Fishwick (Kogan Page in collaboration with Cranfield School of Management). Analyses, among other things, how firms can differentiate themselves from their competitors in bidding situations.

Winning New Business... the Critical Success Factors by Carol Kennedy, Matthew O'Connor and Colin Coulson-Thomas (Policy Publications). Provides hard statistics about what matters most when bidding for new business.

The Seven Deadly Skills of Communicating by Ros Jay (International Thomson Business Press). First chapter provides a practical approach to defining your company's "corporate personality" – the first step to understanding how others see you.

Resource Centre

Institute of Practitioners in Advertising
44 Belgrave Square
London SW1X 8QS
020 7235 7020
www.ipa.co.uk
Leading professional association for advertising agencies

Advertising Agency Register
26 Market Place
London W1N 8AN
020 7612 1200
www.aargroup.co.uk
Source of advice on finding an appropriate advertising agency

Public Relations Consultants Association
Willow House
Willow Place
London SW1P 1JH
020 7233 6026
www.prca.org.uk
Represents many of the larger public relations consultancies

Chartered Institute of Public Relations
32 St James's Square
London SW1Y 4JR
020 7766 3333
www.ipr.org.uk
Many individual public relations professionals belong

Chapter 10

Managing the prospect relationship

Effectively managing relationships with prospective customers pays big dividends in the long term. The more a buyer is aware of your firm's potential at the point when he or she recognises the need for the product or service, the more likely it is you will be invited to tender. If an unknown bidder waits until the point where the buyer is drawing up a short-list before establishing contact, it may be too late. Successful management of prospect relationships means that, even if your firm has not undertaken work for the bidder before, you will be "front of mind" from the very start of the bidding process.

Place more and earlier emphasis on prospective customers' behaviour, emphasis and needs – particularly on likely interactions between the customer and supplier. Involve staff in functions which interact directly with customers. Focus on the internal capabilities of your firm to deliver the right relationship with the prospective customer. Gain a better understanding of the different participants in the value chain.

Key issues

Initial contact with a known prospect is still best undertaken by letter. Telephone calls, faxes and e-mails are usually regarded as an unwarranted use of familiarity if the bidder is unknown personally to the contact. The letter should be brief and to the point and establish a licence for the sender to follow up soon after the letter is received.

The whole point of prospect marketing is to save wasted time and effort by sifting cold calls from potentially warm ones – in other words, the classic "qualifying" of prospects. An initial contact with a prospective client should always be preceded by intelligence gathering which will involve contact with the customer's external stakeholders, particularly users of their products and regulators or "specifiers". For example, in highly complex industries, many manufacturers rely heavily on technical consultants. Even if they are unwilling, for ethical reasons, to reveal inside information about their clients, they can provide valuable insights into the commercial environment in which the company operates.

Recruiting someone to the bid team who has prior contact with the prospect company or inside knowledge of its buying centre is regarded by consistently successful bidders as critical when it comes to managing prospect relationships. When such a relationship is based on mutual respect, the individual effectively has a licence to make personal contact with a key member of the purchasing team. In this case, he or she is worth recruiting for this asset alone. In some cases, this can be achieved by negotiating a joint bid with a local supplier who has already worked with the prospect company (see chapter 13).

Niche players are often effective at prospect marketing because they can develop an international reputation with less investment than big companies and are in a position to anticipate a prospective client's needs well before the tender stage. The success of a computer systems supplier (see case in point on page 63) stemmed largely from its in-depth knowledge of the gas, water and electricity industries.

The most effective form of prospect management is where a bidder anticipates a need that the potential client may not have spotted – thus providing himself with a head start in a field initially free from any competition. This involves using competitive intelligence (see chapter seven) to understand the key business issues potential customers face.

> **Case in point**
>
> A specialist computer systems provider benefited from its policy of building effective relationships with potential customers when it won an £8.5m contract to supply an electricity generation company with new customer and marketing systems against big name competition including leading international IT players and consultants. "It would be unusual for us to go for any tender where we hadn't already been talking to the customer," said the marketing and sales director. "If a company isn't communicating with its potential customers before tenders go out, several other competitors have probably been doing so, and influencing the tender, and therefore your chances of winning are significantly reduced," he added.

Effective use of communications is an important part of this approach. For example, in the IT industry sellers understand well in advance of buyers the impact that new technologies may have on the way companies buy and use computer equipment.

Planning and building your capability to implement the right kind of relationship with prospective customers should be carried out in advance and may involve significant changes to your systems, staff organisation and processes. For example, when customers require service, they expect details of their relationship to be available and used by the person delivering the service. This requires effective internal communication systems. If customers are in contact with several different members of your staff, they also expect the actions of these staff to be coordinated.

Action plan

Your intelligence needs to be good for prospect marketing. The customer will often have an unclear picture of your strengths and you will need a crystal clear picture of it to overcome its tendency to play safe with existing suppliers. Good database management and networking need to be firmly in place before you attempt it.

Desk research is a good place to start. A company's annual report and accounts is a rich source of information but be wary of any creative spin the company might put on its assets and liabilities. Look closely at the figures for retained earnings, capital reserves and issued ordinary shares. Look also at the cash flow of the company and its market value.

The procurement policy of the company is another focus. Some clients are very open with their suppliers while others are more reticent. See if you can spot a buying pattern. Are they tending to concentrate on core activities by outsourcing support functions or do they favour one or two key companies? Do they look for business partners or act as a controlling purchaser? Do they encourage collaboration or competition among suppliers? Is cost or value-added their main criterion?

Unless you can co-opt someone with inside knowledge of the buyer to your bid team (see chapter 16) or collaborate with a bid partner with an existing relationship, your best source of qualitative information will come from other external stakeholders. These might include consultants, former suppliers, key members of professional associations or institutes, local councillors or members of chambers of commerce. If you are pitching for an overseas bid, embassy officials, agency representatives or local agents are useful sources.

All this information will help you, as an outsider, overcome the advantages of familiarity and an established reputation possessed by existing suppliers. The aim of any prospect management is not simply to get yourself added to a "beauty parade" the next time an appropriate bid comes along, but to use your outside perspective to spot needs that existing suppliers are not meeting. This way, you eliminate the threat posed by existing competition.

BOOKSHELF

Handbook of Key Customer Relationship Management by Ken Burnett (FT/Prentice Hall). A comprehensive guide to managing each stage of a customer relationship.

Relationship Marketing for Competitive Advantage: Winning and Keeping Customers by Adrian Payne, Martin Christopher, Helen Peck and Moira Clark (Butterworth-Heinemann). A high-powered team from Cranfield University set out their views on how to make relationship marketing most effective.

Secrets of Customer Relationship Management: a Guide to Getting Much Closer to Your Customers by James G Barnes (McGraw-Hill Education). The emphasis here is how to develop profitable long-term customer relationships.

Relationship Marketing by Merlin Stone and Neil Woodcock (Kogan Page). Excellent primer and practical guide to the essentials of relationship marketing.

Relationship Marketing Strategy and *Building Customer Relationships: best practice*, by Merlin Stone et al (Policy Publications). Two briefings in the *Close to the Customer* series that contain good examples of best practice once a relationship has been initially established with a prospective buyer.

Successful Business Strategy: How to Win in the Marketplace, by Len Hardy (Windrush Books). Part two of this book, covering issues such as "best value", competitive advantage and market leadership, is a good background to developing strategy for prospect relationships.

Resource Centre

Chartered Institute of Marketing
Moor Hall
Cookham
Maidenhead
Berkshire SL6 9QH
Tel: 01628 427500
www.cim.co.uk

Direct Marketing Association
DMA House
70 Margaret Street
London W1W 8SS
020 7291 3300
www.dma.org.uk

Association for the Advancement of Relationship Marketing
www.aarm.org
Useful Web site for those interested in relationship marketing

Call centres

Contact Center World
www.contactcenterworld.com
US website with wealth of information about running call and contact centres.

Call and Contact Centre Association
20 Newton Place
Glasgow G3 7PY
0141 564 9010
www.cca.org.uk
Professional body for call and contact centres.

Chapter 11

Identifying potential new customers

It is too easy to see the two functions of procuring and fulfilling new contracts as separate. Yet the very activities that are essential to successful bid management – gathering competitive intelligence, developing and maintaining good reference sites, drafting proposals and exploiting internal networks – are also essential in searching the market-place for new clients. The more synergy that exists between these functions, the more effective the company will be at winning new business.

Successful firms adopt a variety of strategies in winning over new clients, not all of which are mutually exclusive. These include: pitching for a niche contract with a view to building a broader long-term partnership; identifying a potential client's need before they do; using the network and contacts of senior managers as a strategic resource; and re-structuring operations around the needs of specific industries or niches in the market.

Key issues

Use competitive intelligence to spot opportunities for new business and follow up leads assiduously. Pursuing new business in most industries is a mix of grapevine news, competitive intelligence and regular monitoring of the trade press.

Use your senior managers to pave the way. For example, a key function of a major aerospace company's senior executives is to make sure the company is in the game and positioned to do the business when big orders come up for grabs. Getting on the tender list is an administrative function, which comes later on. It is impossible to underplay the importance of building a company's reputation and positioning so that it both attracts invitations to bid and is in a position to know in plenty of time when invitations to tender are likely to be available.

Use a careful analysis of global bidding trends (see chapter 19) to anticipate customer demand before anyone else. To exploit these trends effectively, restructure your company's capabilities around the needs of specific industries or niches. One of the foundations of an international computer company's turnaround was its focus on "industry customer sets" – groups of businesses in, for example, insurance, manufacturing or banking. This approach helped its staff build industry knowledge and expertise and identify particular solutions that were or would be right for a given industry. This approach is not new – what was new was that, within the computer company, it was coordinated worldwide, making the best use of the company's resources.

If a prospective client is a sister division within an organisation which is already your client, it may be wise to treat your new contacts as if they were a totally new prospect. Rivalries between the purchasing functions of different departments is not uncommon so make sure you understand the internal politics before citing internal references.

Where a decision is being made whether or not to bid for a new client's custom, be honest about your capability and current capacity. Situations where a decision not to bid might be wise include: where a excessive workload already exists, where a submission would put you into competition or where you believe you are only being asked to make an addition to a beauty parade or to provide a check price. One wise managing director always asks himself these three key questions before taking up a bid: Does this contract fit the profile of the market we want to be in? Do we have the appropriate infrastructure and people skills for this activity? What are our chances of winning?

Where the bid is informal, the client's timetable can often be quite short. The decision may take days or weeks rather than months. Make sure that you can respond within the period allowed. Consider everything that you will need to put in place if you are going to meet the deadline. If there is a tight time deadline on the bid, try to discover why. If the client needs to commit the expenditure within his or her current fiscal year, for example, you may be able to structure the bid or the payment schedule in a way which helps the client and, thus, improve your chances.

Case in point

Most suppliers aim to form long-term partnerships with clients they regard as strategic to their interests. Sometimes, however, you have to start small in order to get your foot in the door. A leading packaging supplier had no business with a supermarket giant. When the company won a first contract to supply carrier bags, the business was shared with two other firms. But the contract acted as a showcase for the new supplier's real-time consignment management and computerised distribution. Within two years, the newcomer supplied a range of other packaging products to the supermarket chain. Now it captures orders directly from all the chain's stores. It built its business with this supermarket chain to £23m in less than four years.

Action plan

Integrate your sources of competitive intelligence to ensure that work undertaken on existing bids and fulfilling current contracts throws up leads, prospects and contacts that can be used to recruit new customers. Instil a culture of organisational learning, so that there is a free flow of information and no attempt to hog valuable intelligence for internal political gain.

Don't ignore the sharp-end operational activity designed to discover new customers. Techniques include direct mail and telephone calling to identify prospects. Other activities that may generate enquiries and help to identify new customers include: advertising, public relations, speaking at conferences, attending conferences, taking exhibition stands, publishing a company magazine or newsletter and creating an Internet site.

Make sure that there is an effective process in place to record and follow-up all enquiries. Keep information about the outcome of the follow-up on all new enquiries and use that information to inform decisions about future activity on best possible sources of new enquiries and the most effective follow-up techniques. Develop skills in those enquiry generating techniques that prove most fruitful.

Ensure that the board's network and skills are fully utilised. Extend this to non-executive directors so that all directors act as antennae and ground breakers, spotting opportunities that would not be seen further down the organisation and paving the way for bids in cases where an existing relationship with a prospective customer does not exist.

Draw up a matrix-based system for evaluating prospective bids, to ensure that the value of any new contract is assessed systematically. Build into the matrix issues like your firm's ability to comply with the specification, the nature of likely competition, the political situation of the purchaser – with a big and small "p" – the delivery timescale and the firm's ability to implement the contract.

Provide yourself with the financial data you need to assess whether any bid, particularly one in a new industry or niche, will genuinely lead to a steady stream of business or is likely to prove an expensive and resource-heavy one-off. It may pay to take more time to negotiate a more wide-ranging deal than a smaller short-term one.

Bookshelf

Planting Flowers, Pulling Weeds: Identifying Your Most Profitable Customers to Ensure a Lifetime of Growth by Janet Rubio and Patrick Loughlin (John Wiley & Sons). Two former Dell Computer executives draw on their front-line experience to set out a strategy for building business from key customers.

Developing Strategic Customers and Key Accounts…the Critical Success Factors, by John Hurcomb (Policy Publications). Contains case-studies that provide a wealth of good practice in planning and exploiting the early stages of customer relationships.

Market Research: a guide to planning, methodology and research (Kogan Page). Covers most aspects of desk research, questionnaire-based surveys and data analysis. The second edition has a new chapter on "marketing for free" via the Internet.

Winning Major Business, by Alex Weiss and Stephen Willson (Greenfield Publishing). Good on the factors to take into account when considering bids in new territory.

Direct Hit: Direct Marketing with a Winning Edge by Merlin Stone, Derek Davies and Alison Bond (Pitman Publishing). Excellent primer and practical advice on all aspects of direct marketing, including direct mail, telesales and the use of databases to find customer prospects.

Direct mail: best practice by Merlin Stone et al (Policy Publications). A useful briefing in the *Close to the Customer* series which looks at how to make direct mail more effective.

Resource Centre

Direct Marketing Association
DMA House
70 Margaret Street
London W1W 8SS
020 7291 3300
www.dma.org.uk

Chapter 12

Developing bid team leadership

The style of leadership you adopt with your team is critical to the success of the bid. While each team member is focused on specific and immediate tasks, the bid team leader is the only person able to see above the detail to ensure that the collective capability of the team is steered towards meeting the complex and often conflicting needs of the customer, end-user and the customer's internal stakeholders (see chapter 18). The leader's ability to keep this "balcony view" firmly in place, while motivating and inspiring the team through the right challenges and constraints, ensures that the momentum of its efforts is directed towards the right target.

An effective leader acts as a visionary, envisaging how the outcome of the bid might look and how it is possible to reach that point. He or she also acts as a coach, helping individuals and the team as a whole to develop their talents; a supporter, providing the financial and physical resources required by the bid; and a shield, protecting the team from undue interference by the customer or departments in their own company.

Key issues

Break down inhibitions and hidden tensions in a newly formed team through a well-facilitated brainstorm or a well-designed exercise that has nothing to do with the bid (see *Instant Teamwork* under Bookshelf on page 79). Experience shows that this works better than casual socialising in helping team members learn about each other's strengths, respect each other's ways of working and make effective use of each other's ways of looking at problems.

Get a strong sense for the strengths and weaknesses of individual team members (see chapter 16), and provide the appropriate support. For example, highly creative people want freedom in the way they undertake their work and a licence to challenge others. Their value is in coming up with breakthrough solutions but in the process they may seem self-serving and disruptive to others and you may need to act as a peacemaker. Similarly, a reliable "company worker" may find it difficult to fit in with a free wheeling team that requires members to use their initiative. You may need to act as a coach and supporter to help him or her develop this skill.

Bid teams whose members challenge one another's thinking develop a more complete understanding of the choices and a richer range of options. To ensure that the fight is a "good" one, however, you need to control the environment in which it takes place. This includes providing the right data so that members do not waste time arguing over what the facts might be, encouraging the team to come up with a variety of solutions so that choices become less black and white (see case in point on page 76), and creating a common goal so that team members are less likely to see themselves as individual winners and losers. Teams that handle conflict well also use humour to relieve the tension – and you, as leader, may need to set the example.

As a leader, your job is to sequence and pace the work of the team. This does not mean, as many leaders assume, defining the problem and providing the solution, but rather identifying the challenge and "framing" the key questions and issues that the team needs to confront. It does not mean shielding the team from external threats but rather letting it feel the external pressures within a range it can stand. The head of a US consultancy, Donald L Laurie, uses a pressure cooker as an analogy. A leader, he says, needs to regulate the pressure by turning up the heat while also allowing some steam to escape. If the pressure exceeds the cooker's capacity, the cooker can blow up. But nothing cooks without some heat.

> **Case in point**
>
> To avoid "black and white" solutions and help foster a lateral-minded way of working among team members, project leaders bidding for internal funding for experimental projects at a major pharmaceutical company encourage teams to "brainstorm" their responses to four possible outcomes to the bid. First, that the team wins the funding it's looking for. Second, that it wins more. Third, that it wins less. Fourth, that it fails to win any funding but must salvage value from work already undertaken. In this way team members realise that bidding is not a zero-sum game. They take a more holistic view of the bid process and don't see themselves as "winners" or "losers", whatever the outcome.

Just as you act as "internal spokesperson" between team members, act as the "external spokesperson" for the team as a whole – developing the right relationships between collaborators both inside and outside the organisation, the senior management "sponsoring" the bid and the potential customer. Understand the objectives, needs and interests of these stakeholders so as to orchestrate productive communications between them and the team, and to give the team the information it needs to make a successful bid.

Celebrate success. Do this not only at the successful outcome of the bid but at key milestones. A team that functions well responds best to the visible, objective success of what it is doing.

Action plan

Analyse the culture of the team and adopt the appropriate leadership style. Will team members respond best to clear direction and hands-on guidance or are they best left to their own devices once you have set the parameters of the exercise? Are you best deployed as a coach and supporter, counselling and protecting those team members that are not reaching their maximum potential? Or as a shield and resource gatherer, protecting the team from outside interference and providing additional resources when they are needed?

Analyse your team's attitude to you and let it influence your style. Does your status come from being a first among equals, where your technical leadership will play a key role in the success of the bid, and you will be able to communicate with your peers in their own language? Or is your standing based more on your access to the board or other key departments and your ability to provide the team with the strategic context, the resources and the protection it needs?

Bookshelf

100 Greatest Ideas for Effective Leadership and Management by John Adair (Capstone Publishing). Possibly Britain's leading leadership guru gives practical advice on how to become a better leader.

Effective Leadership: How to Make a Winning Team by John Adair (Pan). More advice from Adair, this time with the accent on making teams perform better.

Managing Creative Groups, by John Whatmore (Roffey Park Management Institute). Looks at the role of the team leader in detail and covers tasks such as coaching, supporting, shielding and motivating. Expensive in comparison with the books below.

Managing Live Innovation, by Michel Syrett and Jean Lammiman (Industrial Society/Butterworth Heinemann). This includes chapters on team building, project management and business leadership. There are no specific case-studies on bids but the advice on team leadership is highly relevant.

Organizing Genius, by Warren Bennis (Nicholas Brealey). America's leading guru on leadership uses six case studies of highly creative groups, like the teams who developed the personal computer and who turned around the Disney Corporation, to draw lessons about what makes a good team leader. Bennis concludes that the best thing a leader can do is to encourage team members to discover their own greatness.

Instant Teamwork, by Brian Clegg and Paul Birch (Kogan Page). This book provides a series of exercises, such as ice-breakers and warm-ups, to help leaders create an instant bond in new teams and revitalise old ones. Birch was a senior executive at British Airways during a strike in 1997, so these techniques have been well tried and tested.

Resource Centre

Leadership organisations:

Centre for Leadership Studies
University of Exeter
Crossmead
Barley Lane
Exeter EX4 1TF
01392 413023
www.ex.ac.uk

The Leadership Trust
Weston-under-Penyard
Ross-on-Wye
Herefordshire HR9 7YH
01989 767667
www.leadership.co.uk

Leadership training:

Harlequin Solutions
2 Exmoor Street
London W10 6BD
020 8960 9400
www.solutions.co.uk

Lifecoaching
11 Honeysuckle Gardens
Lymington
Hampshire SO41 0EH
www.lifecoaching.co.uk

Next Step
5 Knighthayes Walk
Devington Park
Exminster
Exeter EX6 8TU
01392 824547
www.nextstepltd.co.uk

Chapter 13

Managing the bid team

Leading a bid team involves creating the right team spirit and motivating team members by defining an understandable set of challenges (see chapter 12). Managing the team involves breaking down these challenges into achievable milestones and obtaining the right resources to help the team achieve them. By setting the parameters of the bid and providing a structure within which members can work, leaders allow the experts in the team to focus exclusively on what they're best at, confident they have access to necessary resources.

The bid manager is the management focus of the bid and leads it by co-ordinating the roles, responsibilities and contributions of all bid team members. Ideally, he or she should be a manager with practical experience of leading cross-functional teams. If the bid manager has responsibility for a particular function, such as sales or customer service, his or her interest and judgement may be coloured by functional responsibilities, constraining the ability to take a "balcony view", vital to leading and managing the team.

Key issues

Training is a key factor. Many companies cite this as important because bids are dynamic in nature and are apt to change mid-cycle. Effective team managers are constantly on the alert to identify problems or opportunities that are beyond the skills of individuals on the team – for example, on the uses of a new product.

Keep the team updated on changing developments. Stay abreast of all latest shifts that will influence costs, pricing, resources, strategy and application.

To help this process, introduce efficient document control. Many seasoned firms use a computerised bid-file system which enables them to keep an accurate record of agreements, understandings and verbal reports. As one bid manager comments: "You can undo much good work and dishearten the team if you let them labour on the obsolete version of a key document because of a verbal conversation they don't know about."

A good bid plan should not place a straitjacket on the way in which the team operates. Rather, it should set out the overall parameters that will help the team manage its own work methods – the timescales for preparing and viewing the tender activities through to submission, and the resources that will be available.

The team should be given the opportunity to evaluate its own performance. The bid manager, in these circumstances, should act as a facilitator and supporter of the process rather than as someone who looks continuously over the team's shoulder.

Ensure that the bid team maintains a balance between technical excellence, commercial viability and customer requirements. Since most of the team members will be specialists, you will be the only person able to take this overview.

If the bid involves teams from more than one company, never forget that this arrangement may have business potential well beyond that of any immediate contract. Manage the relationship with a long-term as well as a short-term perspective.

Where more than one language is involved, the lead company should put the bid together in its mother tongue. However, additional time should be allowed for sequential executive approval from partners.

Support bid teams overseas. There is nothing lonelier than being the member of a bid team working overseas experiencing poor support from the parent company. Rapid response to e-mails, faxes and telephone calls is absolutely vital to keep up morale and maintain the credibility of the team with the customer.

Case in point

When an advertising agency won the account for a high-profile advertising campaign to launch a new credit card in a head-to-head battle with a market-leading agency, it put much of its success down to team management. The key success factor was not just an excellent team spirit – "the client felt we had energy, motivation and enthusiasm," said the agency's chairman – but the way bid managers acted as resource gatherers for the team, enabling the agency to gain the understanding it needed to outshine the rival agency. "The client was impressed by the volume and quality of work we produced in a short time, and by our grasp of the brand," the chairman said.

While there may be an argument for providing a bonus or incentive to help motivate team members, this should only form part of a larger strategy to promote a strong team spirit. Companies which have a track record of successful bids do not rate this measure very highly (see *Winning New Business...the Critical Success Factors* under Bookshelf on page 85).

Action plan

Start the bonding process right away and maintain it throughout the bid. Don't plunge immediately into the details of the bid but use an unrelated assignment to give each member an insight into how the others work. Celebrate success and key milestones. Provide a framework in which the team can work effectively.

Use your "balcony view" to keep members updated about developments on the bid, ensure that an efficient system of document control is in place (see chapter five) and co-opt whatever additional resources or expertise the team feels it needs.

Look beyond the immediate confines of the bid and plan a debriefing session. Even if the bid is not successful, ensure that the team conducts a proper audit on what it learned about the purchaser and earmark talented team members for future bids. This way, both the company and the team will free themselves from a "win or lose" mentality that often proves detrimental to morale.

Bookshelf

The Big Book of Team Building Games: Trust Building Activities; Team Spirit Exercises and Other Fun Things to Do by John Newstrom and Ed Scannell (Pfeiffer Wiley). Plenty of activities to break the ice and get a team working together.

Building Your Team, by Rupert Eales-White (Kogan Page in association with The Sunday Times). A basic guide to team management, a little short on good examples but with plenty of techniques and tools.

Winning New Business… the Critical Success Factors, by Carol Kennedy, Matthew O'Connor and Colin Coulson-Thomas (Policy Publications). Contains a detailed chapter on managing bid teams, based on a survey of companies with a track record of winning bids.

Winning Major Business by Alex Weiss and Stephen Willson (Greenfield Publishing). Contains useful sections on managing bid teams and supporting them with the right technology.

Resource Centre

Organisations that provide consultancy or training on teams include:

Belbin Associates
3-4 Bennell Court
West Street
Comberton
Cambridge CB3 7DS
01223 264975
www.belbin.com
Consultancy founded by leading teamworking guru Meredith Belbin.

Cambridge Online Learning
BBIC
Innovation Way
Wilthorpe
Barnsley

South Yorkshire S75 1JL
01226 321717
www.cambridge-online-learning.co.uk

High Force Training
21-23 Market Place
Barnard Castle
Co Durham DL12 8NE
0870 162 0789
www.highforce.co.uk

People in Charge
55 Henley Avenue
Oxford OX4 4DJ
01865 396592
www.peopleincharge.co.uk

Chapter 14

Defining and managing a contract bid budget

There is always a cost in winning bids, and it is vital to create a balance between the cost of a bid and the chances of winning the business. Most successful companies focus their bid budgets on proposals where they stand either a better than evens chance of winning or where the potential customer is of special strategic importance. Giving a bid team a budget underscores the importance of their work and provides them with a degree of freedom to approach the bid in the way they deem most effective.

The critical success factor, says one construction bid manager, is knowing that the cost of the bid is worth the value of the potential business – and that you have a good chance of winning against the competition. That way you know you don't waste costly resources on a fruitless proposal. In a big corporation, provision of a substantial dedicated budget is an encouraging sign of top management support and a powerful incentive to the bid team that its work is vital to the company's strategy.

Key issues

Decide whether you need an annual budget to cover all bids over a year or whether you need to define a separate budget for each bid. Much will depend on the profile and size of your company's bids – larger bids generally call for dedicated budgets. Be prepared to add extra budget when you're targeting strategically significant business. The extra cost could be the investment needed to break into a new market.

With limited preparation time, you need to tread a fine line between too much and too little detail in defining your budget. Trust the bid manager to use his discretion on applying resources sensibly.

Once accurately costed, the budget needs to be carefully monitored throughout the bidding process. For a variety of reasons, bidding costs can easily spiral out of control and wreck the initial calculations on which the bid was based.

There are standard costs to all bidding procedures that enable you to cut the preparation time and these, together with available resources, should be regularly updated. Such costs would include, for example, employment overheads – not forgetting such items as company cars and personnel insurance – for the core bidding team (which may vary from one person for a £100,000 bid to a sizeable team for a multi-million pound contract), the cost of secretarial services, travel expenses where necessary, personnel insurance, stationery, computers, telephones and other office equipment, unless these are ranked as part of corporate overheads. Export markets present their own costs such as air travel, hotel accommodation, subsistence and reasonable entertainment expenses.

Another standard cost may be your database of information about potential clients and their key decision-makers, which needs regular updating and maintenance, along with your competitive intelligence research about competitors. Some companies also budget for regular entertainment of likely prospects, the results of which are fed back into their prospect database.

Each bid will also have its unique costs to add in – perhaps special advertising, PR services, consultancy advice, engineers' time, and so on. On really major bids, you may need to set up a special base unit for the bid team. On such bids, says one business development manager in the construction business, you just have to spend what it takes: "If you're not going to do it properly, you're better off not doing it at all."

> **Case in point...**
>
> When an international telecom provider's new strategic bids unit was targeting a key $75m US contract, it was given a £250,000 budget for the bid. The size of the budget underscored the strategic significance of winning this high-profile business against entrenched US competitors. The manager who led the bid said the sizeable budget sent a powerful signal of corporate support to the bid team and gave it a sense of flexibility and freedom of action. It meant the bid manager could make cost decisions without constant upward referral and proved a highly motivating factor. The bid was successful.

The shorter the tender period, often the higher the costs to the client because of long working hours for the bidder and less opportunity to look for savings – although this argument often falls on deaf ears and time pressure on bidders continues to increase.

Workforce costs may be controllable by careful decision-making on the number of people required, making sure it is neither too high (leading to inefficiency and perhaps exceeding the client's budget) or too low (making you vulnerable to delivery promises).

Don't forget the cost of paperwork such as proposal publishing.

Private Finance Initiative (PFI) contracts involve producing multiple copies of proposals, which has priced such work beyond many smaller contractors. A major international construction group, pitched for a PFI government contract and found itself having to produce 18 bound documents of 320 pages each. The cost of compiling its proposal – along with the printing – was in the region of £100,000.

Action plan

Prepare a resources plan for both parts of the costing exercise – preparation and implementation. The first part will help to determine the make-up and recruiting of your bid team.

Draw up a standard list of common bidding cost items, based on experience of past projects. This will also, crucially, enable you to assess at an early stage whether a particular bid is worth pursuing.

Draw up a contingency plan to combat over-runs in the preparatory period – the unexpected is always expensive. You may, for example, need to change or bring in a new member of the team to meet a client's objections or wishes.

Bookshelf

Numbers Guide (Economist Books). A primer for anyone who has to deal with numbers as a regular part of their work, this neat little guide explains the recognised techniques for solving financial problems and analysing numerical information of any kind.

Winning the Bid, by Neil Tweedley (FT/Pitman). The chapter on "pricing your offer" includes a detailed section on managing bid budgets.

Resource Centre

Specialist bidding consultants include:

Adaptation
Mill Reach
Mill Lane
Water Newton
Cambridgeshire PE8 6LY
01733 361149

Insight
Morland Hall
Morland
Cumbria CA10 3BB
01931 714714
www.insight-organisation.com

Chapter 15

Developing bid team communication skills

A bid team is only as good as the resources it is able to draw from the rest of the organisation and its skill at putting together information from all parts of the company to aid its bidding strategy. Its ability to interact with its own firms' "gatekeepers", "influencers" and "decision makers" (see chapter 16) to get the support and information it needs is almost as important as its ability to deal with the equivalent managers in the prospective client – and to communicate effectively among its own members.

Create a culture in which people recognise the value of sharing information. In particular, make other departments of the company aware of the need to share information with specialist bid teams. Make a conscious effort to build up the credibility of bid teams among key stakeholder departments.

Key issues

Foster an open culture which encourages team members to share information. Make it clear that it is the responsibility of everyone in the company to provide information needed for a bid in an open and timely way.

When selecting bid team members, ensure that there is at least one "resource investigator". This kind of individual is extrovert, enthusiastic and a good communicator, able to explore opportunities and develop the right contacts. If resources allow, provide communications training to those team members that need it. This is particularly important in the case of specialist staff recruited to analyse and respond to the technological specifications of the bid.

Develop an internal PR strategy. Ensure that the bid is given maximum publicity in your firm's in-house literature and in the internal publications of key suppliers and partners.

Case in point

An aerospace contractor improves its chances of winning bids by formalising communication between its bid team and other parts of the company. A bid team – including a board director, manager, bid writer and representatives of technologies involved – puts a proposal together. Then a "red team" of non-involved senior managers takes over. It uses red pens to "tear the proposal apart". It role-plays the customer as it checks for tender compliance and company strategy. Its critical approach improves the quality of the proposal and chances of winning the contract. Lastly, a "black team" provides a final costing check with the proposal signed off at the highest level.

Ensure that senior managers are committed to the bid and keep them informed of purpose and progress. Use them to support the bid itself, by presenting the offer or selling your company to the client in other ways.

ACTION PLAN

Consider the issues involved in tackling day-to-day communication, both among the bid team and with other staff in the company. Should the bid team work from one location? Is this practical? If not, what other means can be used to improve communication – for example, videoconferencing, the use of an intranet or groupware system? Does the bid management process (see chapter five) take account of the need for communication?

If large cross-company bids form a regular source of income, consider recruiting and training a permanent task force of project leaders capable of harnessing the full resources of the organisation behind every key bid. These managers should possess the skills to work across departments or subsidiaries and the status to rally support from the board when it is needed.

Ensure that the core of any bid team includes people with the negotiating and research skills to make maximum use of competitive intelligence (see chapter seven) and to access key inside information from the company's stakeholder organisations. Use Belbin's team role definitions (see chapter 16) or an equivalent assessment tool to build this competency into team selection techniques.

Make sure everybody knows about good news as soon as possible. But don't hide bad news. Rumours about bad news are usually worse for team morale than the bad news itself.

Bookshelf

The Handbook of Communication Skills by Owen Hargie (Routledge). Substantial 500-page survey of business communication in many different contexts. Useful to have for ready reference.

Social Skills of Interpersonal Communication by Owen Hargie, Christine Sanders and David Dickson (Routledge). Extensive guide to the topic including the social psychology of communication skills.

The Seven Deadly Skills of Communicating by Ros Jay (International Thomson Business Press). Contains useful chapters on communicating within the team, communicating with senior management, communicating with the individual and communication under pressure.

Effective Communication for Managers: Getting Your Message Across by Christine Simons and Belinda Naylor Staples (Cassell). Broad based and practical book which covers most aspects of verbal and written communication. Includes a useful section on communicating messages with the aid of IT.

Organizing Genius: The Secrets of Creative Collaboration, by Warren Bennis and Patricia Ward Biedermann (Nicholas Brealey Publishing). Many of these case-studies of dynamic team projects, like the Disney turnaround and the Manhattan Project, explore how teams rally and marshal their resources.

Resource Centre

Training companies

Organisations providing training in communication skills include:

Capita Learning and Development
17 Rochester Row
London SW1P 1LA
0870 400 1000
www.capita-ld.co.uk

Illumine Training
Vale House
100 Vale Road
Windsor
Berkshire SL4 5JL
01753 866633
www.illumine.co.uk

Popcomm Training
65 Davies Street
London W1K 5DA
020 7514 7904
www.popcomm.co.uk

Chapter 16

Recruiting and training bid team members

Your choice of team members is critical to the success of the bid for two reasons. First, to demonstrate to the customer the full "constituency" of the product or service you are pitching to provide – especially the technical back-up and ongoing advice. Secondly, to demonstrate your company's ability to work effectively as part of a team. Teamwork is a skill in its own right. It can be assessed in prospective team members and considered as one factor during the selection process.

Picking a winning team involves measuring each individual's technical skills and product knowledge as well as the personal qualities that will determine whether he or she can work effectively alongside people with different perspectives and approaches. This does not mean that you should only select like-minded people. You should have a balance of different personalities with the ability to challenge each other (see chapter 12). But, vitally, they should be able to work together in the right spirit and towards a common goal.

Key issues

An effective bid team contains members with a number of core skills. These may include a commercial adviser able to analyse risk and provide in-house legal and contract advice, a financial controller to advise on pricing policy and cash flow, a technical expert to interpret the technical requirements and prepare work estimates, and a project manager who can define the approach taken by the team and write the proposal. While it may not be possible to have every part of the company represented on the team, people who interface regularly with opposite numbers on the customer's team must have the specialist knowledge to answer key questions and respond to customer's concerns.

> **Case in point**
>
> Bob Taylor, who headed the PARC project that created the first personal computer, believed the secret of its success was "hiring the right people and turning them loose". At PARC, the selection process helped build the group. Candidates were interviewed, had to give a talk in front of other team members, field probing questions and respond to comments. Candidates who survived won built-in support from the others who'd grilled them. As Taylor put it: "They became someone who was going to make it fun for the rest of the team."

Most team members can be drawn from experts within your own organisation. However, you may decide to bring in a team from an external organisation to provide vital local knowledge about the client, additional technical expertise or to share in the risk. In these circumstances, sound out the prospective client to make sure there is no objection to a consortium approach. And seek the client's reaction to individual team members – for example, there may have been a bad experience with your potential collaborator.

Interview each potential team member closely enough – if possible, use a formal assessment procedure – to get a feel for how he or she will operate in a team. Each will bring a different set of strengths and weaknesses. A highly creative person who is good at solving problems may also prove obsessive and unwilling to compromise. A solid, reliable team worker who is good at getting things done, may lack drive and prove indecisive in crunch situations. The aim is to achieve a balance of different personalities, where weaknesses are compensated by strengths in others, rather than a homogenous team which may fail to respond imaginatively to the competition.

If you are unable to determine the exact composition of the team, use the same assessment data to anticipate what personality problems are likely to occur – and plan to tackle them in advance.

Action plan

Make sure the team includes members who can combine the necessary technical expertise with "political" nominees who can access key resources from the team's own organisation or who can provide valuable contacts or inside knowledge about the client's needs, the make-up of the customer buying centre and the views of external stakeholders. You may also need key skills such as project management and financial control.

Ensure there is an assessment process in place that takes into account not only the specialist skills and inside knowledge required by the bid team, but the personality and working style of each individual. Try, wherever possible, to ensure a balance that combines people capable of creative problem-solving and shaping ideas with reliable operators capable of putting ideas into practice.

Bookshelf

Easy Step by Step Guide to Recruiting the Right Staff by Chris Dukes (Rowmark). All the basics for anybody who is coming to the task of recruiting staff for the first time.

Building Your Team, by Rupert Eales-White (Kogan Page in association with The Sunday Times). Contains a detailed chapter on recruiting team members and key team roles.

Team Roles at Work, by Meredith Belbin (Butterworth Heinemann). The foremost guru of teamworking, Belbin has identified nine different roles commonly played by managers and professionals in teams. Each has a set of strengths and "allowable" weaknesses. Belbin's assessment tools, set out in this book, are used the world over by front-line project leaders and team managers.

The Complete Idiot's Guide to Recruiting the Right Staff by Arthur R Pell (Alpha Books). Unfortunately titled work which covers the basics of recruitment.

Resource Centre

Chartered Institute of Personnel and Development
151 The Broadway
London SW19 1JQ
020 8612 6200
www.cipd.co.uk
Leading human resources professionals' association with sources of information about recruitment and training.

UK Recruiter
Blue Waters
Elberry Lane
Churston Ferrer
Brixham
Devon TQ5 0JQ
www.ukrecruiter.co.uk

Chapter 17

Developing negotiating skills

The negotiation stage is the last chance in the bidding cycle to influence the customer's decision. Although many successful bidders believe that the customer's mind is usually made up by this stage, there may be opportunities to sway him by "fine-tuning" – being flexible on price, delivery, post-bid maintenance or another aspect of the bid that the customer considers important. Negotiation is a final opportunity to ram home your capacity to add value in comparison with competitors.

Get your bottom-line negotiating strategy worked out before submitting your bid. Select a team of negotiators to match the customer's. Within the parameters of company policy, leave the team to decide what concessions, if any, to make and what is required in exchange. An ideal negotiating strategy leaves the customer with a "comfort zone" – where he has room for manoeuvre on price, delivery or other factors.

Key issues

Successful negotiating depends on work done earlier in the bid cycle. The negotiation stage is the time to "fine-tune" your offer. It is here that you need to know your bottom-line and stick to it. Guarantees of quality, delivery and after-sales support are rated key success factors by companies that consistently win a high proportion of bids they enter. Highlight any potential problems early on so as to be prepared with solutions to them by the negotiating stage.

Be prepared to be flexible on price. In research published in *Winning New Business* (see Bookshelf on page 106), five times as many bidders who win more than three-quarters of their contracts rate this of top importance compared with companies that win less than a quarter of their bids. In the construction industry particularly, price is said to be key in 99.9 per cent of cases. At the same time, remember that clients can be skilled at second-guessing cost-cutters and may negate any flexibility by factoring this into their calculations.

Case in point

When a construction company bid for an NHS hospital refurbishment project, its original £5m tender was the lowest received – but £250,000 over the client's budget. Unless the contractor could find more savings, there would be no job. In response, the construction company value-engineered the project with suggested alternatives to originally specified materials and components – without significantly degrading the spec. It was a big challenge to re-negotiate all aspects of the project but intensive work over three weeks produced acceptable alternatives in 75 per cent of cases. The construction company almost achieved all the cost savings required and won the re-submitted tender.

Always leave a "comfort zone" for the client to feel able to move around on price, delivery or other key factors. The US negotiation guru Ron Shapiro stresses that "the best way to get what you want is to help the other side get what it wants".

Be prepared to walk away if the terms are not right. Apart from big international contracts where only a handful of firms are capable of tendering and, thus, are all represented, be suspicious of clients with more than five contenders on their short-list. They have not done sufficient work on pre-qualifying contenders. Debrief the team in detail, whether you win the bid or not. Learning from failure as well as success is the surest key to future hits.

Action plan

Assess the skills of your negotiating team. Do they need additional training? Get this under way immediately. Right at the start of the bid, work out how you can negotiate to translate the client's wishes into what you can realistically offer. At this stage, you have a chance of getting the client to frame his final specification with your offer in mind.

Identify probable areas of agreement and disagreement between your team and the client's. Your team will need to know whether this is a likely one-off contract or whether a longer-term relationship is possible. In the latter case, more trade-offs may be acceptable.

Remember that the ideal in any negotiating stance is a win/win situation for both you and the client. This is best achieved by paying close attention to the client, trying to understand his agenda, both overt and hidden, and being conciliatory, not aggressive.

Understand the value to the client of each element or component in the bid offer and know exactly what you can give away and what you must retain. Your end position or bottom line must be firmly in your mind at all times.

Concentrate on the key issues and do not be distracted by fine details or clause-by-clause nit-picking. Remember always that a good contract, as bid management consultant Neil Tweedley says, "is one that is put away in a filing cabinet and never needed again".

If you are invited to post-tender negotiations, it is possible that the customer is out to drive a hard bargain with the lowest bidders. It is, therefore, important early on to establish whether there is likely to be a post-tender negotiating stage before structuring your offer price. Tenderers differ on post-tender negotiating policy. Some use it on price on tenders over a certain value, others only use it for clarification. Still others use it where there is no outright winner or there are doubts over some aspect of quality or delivery.

Bookshelf

Understanding and Negotiating Business Contracts: Master the Small Print and Get a Better Deal by Jonathan Rush (How To Books). A basic guide to drawing up contracts and negotiating aimed mostly at small and medium-sized companies that don't have access to expensive lawyers.

Harvard Business Review on Negotiation and Conflict Resolution by various authors (Harvard Business School Press). Essentially a big company view of the subtleties of negotiation in an ever-more complex business world. Collection of papers which have appeared in the *Harvard Business Review*.

Everything is Negotiable, by Gavin Kennedy (Century). Sets out to show that getting a better deal is possible in any situation and includes a section on negotiating overseas.

Managing Negotiations, by Gavin Kennedy, John Benson and John McMillan. (Century Business) Offers a four-phase framework for practical use in avoiding negotiating mistakes.

Getting to Yes, by Roger Fisher, William Ury and Bruce Patton. (Century Business) A global bestseller among guides to negotiation, with practical strategies for getting what you want while leaving the other side happy.

Getting Past No, by William Ury. (Century Business) Sequel to the above, concentrating on those difficult people who aren't willing to do a deal and offering strategies for breaking the deadlock.

Kennedy on Negotiation, by Gavin Kennedy (Gower Publishing). Virtually a business-school course in negotiation skills by the UK's foremost expert in the field. Not an easy read, but it includes not only Kennedy's theories and models but those of competing experts.

Winning New Business…the Critical Success Factors, by Carol Kennedy, Matthew O'Connor and Colin Coulson-Thomas (Policy Publications) Contains a detailed section and model on negotiating, based on a survey of successful bid management in 293 companies in a cross-section of industries.

Winning Major Business, by Alex Weiss and Stephen Willson (Greenfield Publishing). Chapter three, on the tender process, has much sound advice on negotiating teams and procedures.

Resource Centre

Training and consultancy:

Business Skills Training
Fern House
Attenborough
Nottingham NG8 6AQ
0115 922 0330
www.businessskilltraining.co.uk

Canning International Training and Development
10 Knaresborough Place
London SW5 0TG
020 7370 1055
www.canning-ltd.co.uk

John Seymour Associates
Park House
10 Park Street
Bristol BS1 5HX
0845 658 0654
www.john-seymour-associates.co.uk

JS Training
3 Manor Courtyard
Hughenden Avenue
High Wycombe HP13 5RE
01494 446560
www.jstraining.co.uk

OnCourse
1 Downside
Lewes
East Sussex BN7 1EE
0845 230 0035
www.oncourse.co.uk

The Still Point
Anfield House
2 Strickland Place
Southwold
Suffolk IP18 6HN
01502 722538
www.thestillpoint.co.uk

US consultants
All have informative websites and run negotiation training courses

The Negotiation Institute
www.negotiation.com

The Negotiation Skills Company
www.negotiationskills.com

Tradewinds Negotiation Training
www.tradewindsnegotiation.com

Chapter 18

Understanding the role of internal stakeholders

Each company has a unique way of taking its major purchasing decisions – even if it hasn't designed a formal model. Not all internal interests are represented in the customer's buying centre or overtly articulated by the client's front-line team. Penetrating more deeply into the customer company to gain new insight of the important issues at stake is one of the most critical steps in a successful bid.

"To understand someone, you have to stand in his shoes and walk about in them a bit," says the small-town lawyer hero of Harper Lee's *To Kill a Mockingbird*. To present the winning argument, the bidder needs to acquire sufficient inside information to understand not only the contribution of individuals formally on the buying team but the internal stakeholders inside the company who have an interest – and thus an influence – in the outcome of the tender.

Key issues

Always include someone on the bid team with a good knowledge of the customer, even if his or her knowledge of the product or service offered is minimal. Companies with a successful track record of winning bids stress the importance of having someone with inside skill at identifying the most important individuals on the purchase team, understanding the customer's mission, objectives and markets, and understanding the cost factors most likely to influence the final choice of supplier.

Identify the key stakeholders, who may or may not be represented on the purchase team. Most commonly, these will include senior managers, whose reputations may be on the line, particularly if the project is high profile; the "client" who is paying the bill and expecting a return on his investment (often an internal department but sometimes an external client of the purchaser); and the "end-user" of the product or service who, if not the actual customer, will have needs that the customer must take into account.

Once you have established which internal stakeholders exert a key influence, take each in turn and ask the question: what do they get out of this deal? Try to understand the concerns of different groups of stakeholders and address them both in your proposal and the way you communicate with the different groups.

When targeting a communication campaign at the client's buying centre (see chapter four), do not forget the internal stakeholders. "Gatekeepers" – for example secretaries and professional purchasing personnel who control the flow of information to the buying centre – may play an important role in the early stages of the purchase decision, particularly if you are unknown to the client. They are just as influenced as the actual decider by a sales campaign that establishes the bidder's credibility.

Seek external help if you are bidding to an overseas customer. The stakeholders are likely to be less immediately obvious. You may, for example, be required to overcome political resistance, either from within the government in whose country you are trying to bid, or from local representatives with their own motives. Embassy officials and local agents are likely candidates to approach.

Another stakeholder, often overlooked, is represented by the customers of your own customer. These can be external customers who are the consumers of the products or services your customer supplies, or they can be internal customers, who are either part of your customer's organisation or in some way directly affiliated to it. Your customer's key accounts are very important to them and can exert considerable pressure on the way they operate. Find out who are the most influential and target them for support.

> **Case in point**
>
> A construction company with a particularly progressive outlook on management seeks to engage all stakeholders in some of its major building projects through a partnership approach. Partnering with other stakeholders delivers a range of benefits – better understanding of the client's needs; rapid and accurate information flow; early identification of problems and integrated approach to solutions; faster and more flexible problem solving; faster building and better co-ordinated services work; less wasted meetings and time on site; and reduction in design and building costs.

ACTION PLAN

When building your database of information about a prospective customer, include the key stakeholders in the company's procurement policy. These will include gatekeepers (see above), users or "internal customers" (people who will use the product or benefit from the service being purchased), "influencers" (the technical staff, subject experts and senior executives who shape the bid specification) and "deciders" (the managers who have the formal and informal power to select the final supplier).

Use your inside information to find out which of these formal stakeholders are represented on the buying team and which ones exercise an external influence. Take each in turn and analyse what their view of your firm is likely to be and whether they are likely to prove an inside source of support for your bid. If a stakeholder group and its probable influence is sizeable, consider an advertising or communications campaign targeted solely at it.

BOOKSHELF

Making Rain: the Secrets of Building Lifelong Client Loyalty by Andrew Sobel (John Wiley and Sons). Aimed at large companies and service firms who want to build long-term relationships with their customers. Looks at how to understand what customers really want.

Managing Key Clients by Kevin Walker, Cliff Ferguson and Phil Denvir (Thomson Learning). Looks at how to get inside the minds of decision-makers in key clients and understand how to influence them into the future.

Loyalty Rules! How Today's Leaders Build Lasting Relationships by Frederick Reichheld (Harvard Business School Press). Bain Consultancy director looks at the key ingredients of customer loyalty. Useful for giving perspective on how to approach understanding what customers want.

Profitable Customers: How to Identify, Develop and Keep Them, by Charles Wilson (Kogan Page in association with the Institute of Directors). A book based on how to identify profitable customers and ensure that they receive the most attention and service. It contains several sections on how to influence internal stakeholders.

Relationship Marketing Strategy and *Relationship Marketing: the technology* by Merlin Stone et al (Policy Publications). Two briefings in the *Close to the Customer* series. The first contains a number of relevant sections, including planning effective customer management relationships and a quick guide to segmented relationships. The second looks at how to use IT effectively to develop relationship management.

Resource Centre

Cardiff Business School
Aberconway Building
Colum Drive
Cardiff CF10 3EV
029 2087 6013
www.cf.ac.uk/carbs
Runs MBA on buyer behaviour and the market-place.

Chapter 19

Understanding global bidding trends

Spotting the emergence of new markets and gaining information about them is important when you come to define your product's value in the terms that customers in overseas markets might expect (see chapter three). This is all the more important because, in many industries, future competition may come from unexpected quarters, while future demand will be generated in new markets. A shrinking customer base in developed countries caused by mergers and acquisitions may be off-set by new customers from emerging economies – both trends leading to a change in the current rules of the game.

World markets are becoming increasingly complex and sophisticated. Often, the richest prizes go to those who spot key trends first and act to seize advantage from them. Develop an outward looking culture that encourages senior managers to look beyond the confines of existing markets for new opportunities.

Key issues

In formulating your company's strategic plans for international competition, develop a way of differentiating between key characteristics in each country you target. These should include: the foreign trading attitude of the government (free trade or closed protectionism?); the taxation system (what effect will differing import duties, commodity taxes and corporate taxes have on your company's bottom line?); and infrastructure (what efficiency, delivery time and cost can you reasonably expect given the state of the harbours, railways, highways, telephones, mail, road transport and storage facilities?).

Examining the foreign trading attitude of the government in detail should give you many clues as to likely bidding opportunities. Specific questions might include: is the government pursuing a strategy of economic growth? (in which case, the opportunities for state or privately-funded infrastructure projects will rise together); is this growth strategy predicated on encouraging greater foreign investment? (in which case, tax and regulatory systems will favour foreign bids for local projects); and is the government actively fostering specific local industries through tax breaks and subsidies? (in which case, local competition will play a role in key bids as well as overseas firms).

Equal scrutiny should be focused on the direct competitors you face in the overseas market you are targeting. Specific questions might include: What is your current market share (at home and in the target country) and how do you rank? What market share does each of your competitors have? How good are their sales and marketing strategies? What areas of R&D are they engaging in? Which industries are at the growth stage in the life-cycle of their products and which are at saturation?

Critically, you also need to look at the future make-up of the global competition you are likely to face. Specific questions here include: Which competitors are the strongest and can be expected to be the most aggressive against your efforts? Which have formidable or perhaps substantial hidden financial strength to take over the market you are in? Which are pursuing strategies of horizontal or vertical integration that will make them more efficient and enable them to draw on greater resources in many major bids?

Look at potential entrants who could pose a future threat. To be effective in defending and protecting your market position, both at home and abroad, you need to ask yourself the following questions: Which foreign countries are most aggressive in entering your domestic markets? Which of your domestic competitors might be most susceptible to the efforts of foreign entrants – would you also be on their target list? What type of technology or superior products are they likely to bring into your market?

> **Case in point**
>
> Globalisation creates competitive markets on a world scale – for example, British, French and Japanese construction companies compete as readily for contracts in Hong Kong or the Gulf States, as for projects in their own countries. But globalisation also brings together natural competitors in consortia to win international bids. Such consortia are often cross-border – for example a consortium that won the contract to upgrade telephone networks for the British armed services (see chapter 20). Massive regrouping of companies is also giving individual countries more of a chance to win lucrative defence contracts, as in Italy, where the two top manufacturers of military aircraft merged to create a more effective Italian competitor in world markets.

Finally, you need to turn the spotlight on yourself and examine how well equipped you are to defend your position. Have you invested in sufficient R&D to counteract the influx of new products and services? Are your key products and services sufficiently protected by internationally recognised patents and contractual rights? Where you have gaps and weaknesses in your ability to take part in key global bids, have you forged relationships with friendly firms at home or competitors abroad that will allow you to form a consortium or counter one forged by a rival in the same bid?

Action plan

When developing your capability to gather competitive intelligence, include the key economic indicators of countries and regions in which you have a direct interest. Extend this to include any change in government, developments in trade regulation and public policy and any trade agreements that govern the whole region.

When investigating each likely competitor in any country or region, assess also its value as a collaborator or a partner in a consortium bid. Include up-and-coming local firms that could make an effective partner in joint ventures based on their local knowledge and networks and your technological expertise.

When assessing international players in your industry or market-place, factor in what likely impact they would have as an entrant in your domestic market. Consider whether you would be better off forming an alliance with them or mounting a defensive strategy, perhaps in conjunction with other local firms.

In developing a global strategy, consider whether you are likely to be the hunter or the hunted in the welter of mergers and acquisitions that are currently taking place. Are you better off staying in specific niches or pursuing an aggressive game of growth to enable you to compete for bids against the bigger players?

Bookshelf

Corporate Strategies for a Borderless World, by Jan Bossak and Soichiro Nagashima (Asian Productivity Organisation, Tokyo). Surprisingly accessible, despite using highly scientific diagnostic tools, this guide starts from basics and works upwards in developing the complex strategies needed to compete in a global marketplace.

Guide to Economic Indicators (Economist Books). Covers all the essential indicators including GNP and GDP, growth, trends and cycles, investment and savings, balance of payments, exchange rates and financial markets.

Understanding Global Business (Institute of Directors). A basic guide to doing business abroad for the medium-sized company, with contributions from the British Exporters Association and the Institute of Export. The chapter on breaking into new markets is particularly relevant to international bidders.

Global Teams: How Top Multinationals Span Boundaries and Cultures with High-speed Teamwork by Michael J Marquard and Lisa Horvath (Davies-Black Publishing). Looks at best practice from global leaders such as General Motors University and Colgate-Palmolive.

Resource Centre

For information about exporting:

British Exporters Association
Broadway House
Tothill Street
London SW1H 9NQ
020 7222 5419
www.bexa.co.uk

Institute of Export
Export House
Minerva Business Park
Lynch Wood
Peterborough PE2 6FT
01733 404400
www.exportorg.uk

International Chamber of Commerce (UK)
12 Grosvenor Place
London SW1X 7HH
020 7838 9363
www.iccuk.net

For information about specific export markets

Economist Intelligence Unit
26 Red Lion Square
London WC1 4HQ
020 7576 8181
www.eiu.com
Publishes individual country and market guides

Chapter 20

Pitching against international competitors

Bidding for business becomes more complex when international competitors enter the ring. While a company may understand the strategies and tactics that home-grown competitors use, it may be unfamiliar with those employed by foreign competitors. And as globalisation gathers pace, bidding for business – whether at home or abroad – increasingly involves taking on overseas rivals.

Understand the new factor that competing against international competitors brings to the game. In an overseas market where your company's strengths may not be known, establish your firm's credibility early enough to become a contender for the short-list. Focus your attack in areas where the competition does not want to compete or has the resources to do so. Ally your company with effective partners – who carry clout in their own home markets.

Key issues

Ensure there is a match with your corporate plan in the region you are bidding. The business plan should focus on existing or latent volume markets, while not neglecting your domestic market. That said, if the opportunity represents a strategic initiative for your company, separate the cost-price relationship in your bid. But if you are to withstand potential losses in one area to make money somewhere else, you require strength in depth.

Count the cost before you commit yourself. Bidding on an international front is expensive. A telecom provider's successful bid for a $75m systems contract from a leading US car manufacturer (see chapter 14) was preceded by a two-month marketing offensive, with tailored PR and advertising messages designed to answer the question: why was the telecoms provider in the US market?

Alliances help open the door to a bidder unknown in the region – but only with a company that counts. One consortium comprising of a UK telecoms provider, a US defence group and and a UK engineering conglomerate beat off an all-UK consortium to win a £1bn contract to supply upgraded telephone networks to the British armed services because the consortium had an effective combination of world-class technical skills and detailed knowledge of how the British government works. By contrast, an international consortium was eliminated from the bid to supply combat aircraft to the US Joint Strike Fighter programme (see case in point) because the same synergy of local knowledge and technical expertise did not exist.

In this sense, success in international bidding often comes down to which company or consortium has the best networks of contacts and support. These may be needed to overcome political resistance either from within the government of the country where you are bidding or from local representatives with their own motives. In some countries, you will also need to deal with business practices that would be considered unacceptable in more developed states. Advice from local and overseas government staff, embassy officials or local agents can often prove invaluable.

For all these reasons, project managers on international bids require stakeholder management skills not required on local bids. For example, a manager working for a computer systems company was asked to take over a stalled international project to introduce a computerised typesetting and layout facility for a major national

> **Case in point**
>
> Bidding against international competitors requires a combination of good networking and playing to your unique strengths. One major aerospace company lost one of the "peach" bids in the defence industry – a $100bn contract to supply combat aircraft to the US Joint Strike Fighter programme – because its choice of consortium partners did not give it a local edge with the US government. But it compensated for the loss with a £1bn Australian order for supply and maintenance of trainer aircraft, and a further £500m contract to supply aircraft to the Gulf state of Qatar. Its international competitive edge comes partly from its ability to integrate different technological systems used by air forces that have grown piecemeal – a "black art" that makes or breaks modern defence programmes as well as the ambitions of companies that bid for them.

newspaper. He had to contend not only with meeting the expectations of the client and the senior management within his own company, who regarded the project as vital to the company's reputation, but with the difficulties of keeping the project team in touch with each other, (whose members included both American and European advisers), and with managing the views of an international advisory board set up by the government two years before to ensure the editorial objectivity of the publication.

The best way of making an impact in an international bid is to concentrate on areas where competitors cannot or do not want to compete. A good example is bids supported by international lending agencies like the European Bank for Reconstruction and Development and the Asian or African development banks. These are often able to provide products and services which are not available locally or to transfer badly needed knowledge or expertise. Another is aerospace/defence bidding where the skill of integrating different technological systems is proving a worldwide commodity (see case in point on page 123).

Bidding against international bidders, ironically, often provides you with an early opportunity to meet face-to-face with your opponents in a way not often available in local bids. Many high-profile international bids, particularly those supported by funding agencies or government departments, bring together all potential bidders in a pre-bid meeting to elaborate upon any special needs they may have and to highlight various points of the project. This not only provides you with an opportunity to enhance your knowledge of the client but to size up the opposition. On an international bid, this may seem more difficult as competitors may be represented by local agents. For this reason, you should involve your own local contacts whose first-hand knowledge may lead them to note something important that you miss.

Action plan

Ensure that any matrix used to assess the value of new bids (see chapter 11) builds in the additional cost and greater complexity of international bids. Assess carefully how much investment you will need to raise the profile of your firm and acquire the specialist knowledge to give yourself a fighting chance of making the short-list.

Build up the right networks in advance. Include embassy and British Council officials, contacts in the right development agencies, local suppliers, officials in local government and, if appropriate, journalists from local publications and broadcasting stations.

Identify companies that might make imaginative partners in a consortium bid. These could include firms in your own country which have better contacts in the host region or expertise that you lack, international competitors who also want to expand their commercial presence in the host region, or local firms in the host region wanting to trade their knowledge and contacts for your technological expertise.

Build up a "hit" team of project managers capable of managing large or complex international bids. Ensure that they have the linguistic, diplomatic and leadership skills needed to manage an international team that may include representatives from other firms or stakeholder organisations. Ensure they have the status or authority to draw on resources from across the whole company.

Review your code of ethics to take into account the different attitudes to business negotiations and collaboration in developing regions. Draw a clear line, for example, between what you see as acceptable hospitality in a country where different traditions apply and unacceptable corruption that will compromise your firm either at home or in the eyes of the international business community.

Bookshelf

Competitive and Ethical: how business can strike a balance, by Giles Wyburd (Kogan Page). The chapter on the difficult area of bribery and entertaining is particularly relevant to international bids in developing countries.

International Business Culture, by Terry Garrison (ELM Publications). A very insightful book which examines how a country's business culture is shaped through economic ideology, public policy, history and religion and then explores their impact through a series of case-studies including the alliance between Renault and Volvo, the 1994 Mexican currency devaluation and the Channel high-speed rail link.

International Management: a guide to cross-cultural business, by John Mattock (Institute of Directors). Although international bidding only gets a small reference, this book is very good on issues surrounding language, culture and different attitudes to business.

Riding the Waves of Culture: Understanding Cultural Diversity in Business by Fons Trompenaars and Charles Hamden Turner (Nicholas Brealey Publishing). Encourages readers to understand their own culture before doing business with others.

Resource Centre

Organisations that can aid companies moving into overseas markets:

British Exporters Association
Broadway House
Tothill Street
London SW1H 9NQ
020 7222 5419
www.bexa.co.uk

Institute of Export
Export House
64 Clifton Street
London EC2A 4HB
020 7247 9812
www.export.org.uk

International Chamber of Commerce (UK)
12 Grosvenor Place
London SW1X 7HH
020 7838 9363
www.iccuk.net

Department of Trade and Industry
Response Centre
1 Victoria Street
London SW1H 0ET
020 7215 5000
www.dti.gov.uk

Trade Partners UK
www.tradepartners.co.uk
Government body that helps companies sell overseas. Website contains searchable database of other websites of use to exporters.

Chapter 21

Developing and using reference sites

Praise or commendation from a third party can be a powerful influencer with potential customers. Of course, you make claims about the effectiveness of your own products and services. Where such claims are independently verified by users they carry substantially more weight. Increasingly, purchasers of major products or services consider track record as an important indicator of the value a potential supplier can deliver. The picture of a company's track record is highly coloured by the views existing users express about it.

Consider the impact either formal or informal references have on your ability to make sales in the future. Develop formal reference sites that can become "best-practice beacons" for future customers. Don't ignore the impact that "grapevine gossip" may have on how potential customers perceive your company's track record.

Key issues

Developing agreed reference sites on which bidders can draw at critical stages of the bid is a major research exercise, requiring additional negotiating skills to establish client cooperation.

Consider the different ways in which a reference site can be used. These include for potential customer visits, as a customer reference in a brochure or on an Internet site, as a formal case study published in company literature or a house magazine, and as a press release or feature article issued to the trade or technical press. A potential reference site may be willing to cooperate in some or all of these activities – it's important to determine which.

The willingness of any customer to act as a referee in a future bid, either directly or indirectly, should be negotiated well in advance. Be clear about exactly what references the customer is willing to give. Understand how much resource – chiefly in terms of time – the customer is prepared to devote to receiving visits and talking to your potential customers. Bear in mind that the reference site will hope to obtain some benefit as well as your firm. Decide what that benefit should be – possibly improved service, extra discounts.

Ideally, bidders should be able to draw on a variety of referees that can be deployed flexibly to fit different circumstances. For example, it may be important to find a reference site in the same or similar industry as a prospective customer. Alternatively, the reference site may need to have faced a similar business or technical problem as the prospective customer. Understanding what is important to the prospective customer and then dealing with that issue at the reference site is an especially powerful way of underscoring your company's capabilities.

If the reference is to take the form of a written case study of a past contract, clients will usually require "sight of copy" before approving the text. If they are likely to be approached by your next potential client during the evaluation process, this also needs to be cleared with them in advance, along with the context in which their remarks are to be placed.

A good case study, like an article, tells a story. It should place the contract in the context of the client's strategic circumstances, emphasise the reason why both the bid and the implementation of the project were a success in terms of the bidding firms'

> **Case in point**
>
> A computer service company's successful bid to become a key service provider to a larger direct supplier of PCs, rested heavily on the PC supplier's ability to "reference" the computer service company's infrastructure, quality of service and European capability. This proved a critical part of the PC supplier's informal "hands off" evaluation that preceded close contact between the prospective project teams. The PC supplier sought a partner with European and international capability to build its business internationally and to provide a continuity of service around Europe and beyond – in Australia, Mexico and North America. As the computer service company's managing director explained, word of mouth references were critical. "Bidders who can establish good references move quickly to the front of the customer's consideration."

strengths and capabilities and reflect the client's perspective of the relationship as well as your own. Ideally, it should be based on a mixture of desk research drawn from the client's and supplier's corporate literature and relevant business articles, and attributable comments from key managers from both the client's and supplier's project teams. Again, any attributed quotations or reference needs to be agreed and cleared with the individuals concerned.

A supporting reference is like a good capability statement. It should be created for the occasion, supporting specific arguments or claims made in the tender documentation or the formal proposal. However, much of the groundwork for the reference can be done in advance. The basic text can be drafted and cleared with clients well in advance, making amendments and alterations quicker once the main purpose of the reference becomes known. If case-study material is likely to be used frequently, there may be an argument for having it professionally researched and written by marketing staff or an independent business writer with front-line journalistic experience.

Do not overlook the reference impact that other users of your products or services may have. The "grapevine gossip" factor is not to be underestimated in many industries. Deal with the legitimate concerns of all customers and pay particular attention to making sure that you handle complaints effectively.

Action plan

Whenever a project has been successfully completed or renewed, ensure that it is part of the front-line staff's basic procedure to enquire whether the client would be happy to act as a referee in future bids. Ensure also that they are aware of the sensitivity and ethical considerations that may be involved in obtaining consent.

Make researching and drafting case study material for reference sites an additional responsibility of the department or external agency responsible for drawing up corporate literature and capability statements. Ensure that they have the research and interpersonal skills required.

Regularly review the material in the light of changing circumstances. Maintain an ongoing liaison with the relevant managers in the client firm, even if you no longer undertake work for them. Review how you handle customer complaints and take action to develop more effective business processes for handling complaints alongside action to address the sources of the most common and troublesome complaints.

Bookshelf

Style Guide: the best-selling guide to English usage (Economist Books). Developed from the style manual used by The Economist, this guide will help researchers of bidders' reference sites write lively and concise case-study material.

Managing complaints and compliments by Merlin Stone et al (Policy Publications). A briefing in the *Close to the Customer* series which explores how to set up business processes that handle complaints effectively.

Resource Centre

BrainSells UK
3 Kingslawn Close
London SW15 6QJ
020 8789 4336
www.brainsells.com
Consultancy that advises on reference selling

Writers who write case studies include the authors of this book:

Peter Bartram
The Bartram Partnership
01273 565505
peter@bartrampartnership.co.uk

Carol Kennedy
020 8947 6626 cak@dircon.co.uk

INDEX

4-Consulting, 46

Adair, John, 78
Adaptation, 31, 91
Advanced Business Facilities, 46
Advertising Agency Register, 60
African Development Bank, The, 36
Alliance of International Market Research Institutes, 21
Amacom, 51
Association for the Advancement of Relationship Marketing, 67
Aziz Corporation, 13

Bain Consultancy, 112
Baker, John S, 44
Barnes, James G, 65
Belbin Associates, 85, 94
Belbin, Meredith, 100
Bennis, Warren, 78, 95

Benson, John, 106
Bensoussan, Babette, 44
bid team
   recruiting members, 97-101
bid team management, 81-86
bidding process, 28-32
bidding skills
   bid team budget, 87-91
   bid team leadership, 74-80
   bid team management, 81-86
   bid team recruitment, 97-101
   bidding process, 28-32
   communication skills, 92-96
   company survey, 4-7
   competitive intelligence, 41-47
   competitors, international, 121-128
   customer buying centres, 22-27
   customers, new, 68-73

global bidding trends, 114-120
internal stakeholders, 109-113
negotiating, 102-108
presentations, 9-14
product messages, 55-60
product value, 15-21
proposals, 48-54
prospect relationships, 61-67
reference sites, 128-132
tender documents, 33-40
Birch, Paul, 79
Birn, Robin, 19
Bond, Alison, 73
Bossak, Jan, 118
BrainSells UK, 132
British Airways, 79
British Council, 124
British Exporters Association, 118, 119, 127
British Market Research Association, 20
British Standards Institution, 40
Budd, Stanley, 38
Burnett, Ken, 65
Burwell, Helen P, 44
Business Data Consulting, 46
Business Skills Training, 107

buying centres, 22-27
BS5750 standards, 30, 35, 38

Cadbury-Schweppes, 59
Call and Contact Centre Association, 67
Calyx Communications, 53
Cambridge Online Learning, 86
Canning International Training & Development, 107
Capita Learning & Development, 96
Cardiff Business School, 113
Centre for Leadership Studies, 79
Chapman, Colin, 44
Chartered Institute of Marketing, 19, 20, 66
Chartered Institute of Personnel Development, 100
Chartered Institute of Public Relations, 60
Chartered Institute of Purchasing and Supply, 27
Christopher, Martin, 65
Cincom Systems, 32
Clark, Moira, 65
Clegg, Brian, 79

Colgate-Palmolive, 118
communication skills, 92-96
competitive intelligence, 41-47
contract bid budget, 87-91
Contract Center World, 67
Corrigan, Paul, 38
Coulson-Thomas, Colin, 31, 32, 59, 106
Coulter Ford Associates, 14
Cranfield School of Management, 59
Cranfield University, 65
customers
   identifying new, 68-73

Daimler, 59
Davidson, Hugh, 59
Davies, Derek, 73
de Forte, John, 52
Dell Computers, 72
Denvir, Paul, 112
Department of Trade & Industry, 128
Dickson, David, 95
Direct Marketing Association, 67, 73
Disney Corporation, 78
Dukes, Chris, 100

Eales-White, Robert, 84, 100

Economist Intelligence Unit, 120
Emphasis Training, 53
EMP Intelligence Service, 47
Ernst, Carl R, 44
European Bank for Reconstruction & Development, The, 36, 39, 124
European Federation of Associations of Market Research, 21
European Institute of Purchasing Management, 27
European Union, 35, 37, 38, 39

Ferguson, Cliff, 112
Fiat, 59
Fisher, Roger, 106
Fishwick, Frank, 59
Fleischer, Craig S, 44
Forum Corporation, The, 26
Forsyth, Patrick, 52
Freed, Richard C, 51
Freed, Sherrin, 51
Friedman, George, 44
Friedman, Meredith, 44

Garrison, Terry, 126
General Motors, 118

global bidding trends, 114-120
globalisation, 1

Hague, Paul, 19
Hamden Turner, Charles, 126
Hardy, Len, 19, 66
Hargie, Owen, 94, 95
Harlequin Solutions, 80
Hayes, Mike, 38
Hertz, 16
High Force Training, 86
Horvath, Lisa, 118
Hurcomb, John, 72

Industrial Society, The, 13
Illumine Training, 96
Insight, 52, 91
Institute of Directors, The, 38, 112
Institute of Export, The, 118, 119, 127
Institute of Practitioners in Advertising, The, 60
internal stakeholders, 109-113
International Chamber of Commerce, The, 119, 127
international competitors, 121-127
ISO 9000, 35, 38

Jackson, Peter, 19
Jay, Antony, 12
Jay, Ros, 59, 95
John Seymour Associates, 107
Jones, Guy, 52
Joyce, Paul, 38
JS Training, 107
Juniper Consultancy Services, 47

Kahaner, Larry, 45
Kennedy, Carol, 26, 59, 85, 106, 132
Kennedy, Gavin, 105, 106
Kwakye, A A, 38

Lammiman, Jean, 78
Laurie, Donald L, 76
leadership, 74-80
Leadership Trust, The, 79
Lee, Harper, 109
Leigh, Andrew, 13
Lifecoaching, 80
LMA Sales Training & Consultancy Services, 54
Local Government Information Unit, 39
Local Government Association, 39
Loughlin, Patrick, 72

Market Research Society, The, 20
Marsh, P D V, 38
Marquard, Michael J, 118
Mattock, John, 126
McCann, Deiric, 50, 51
McMillan, John, 106
Moore, Geoffrey A, 26

Nagashima, Soichiro, 118
National Book Network, 44
National Health Service, 103
Naylor Staples, Belinda, 95
negotiating skills, 102-108
Negotiation Institute, The, 108
Negotiation Skills Company, The, 108
Newstrom, John, 84
Next Step, 80

O'Connor, Matthew, 26, 59, 85, 106
Oncourse, 108

PARC, 98
Pareto Law, The, 8
Patler, Louis, 59
Patton, Bruce, 106
Payne, Adrian, 65

Peck, Helen, 65
Pell, Arthur, R, 100
People in Charge, 86
Popcomm Training, 96
Prentice Hall, 44
Presentation Business, The, 14
presentations, 9-14
Private Finance Initiative, 89, 90
Proctor & Gamble, 59
products
   key messages, 55-60
Proposal Group of Len Duffy & Associates, The, 53
proposals, 40-54
Public Relations Consultants Association, 60

reference sites, 129-134
Reichheld, Frederick, 112
relationship management, 61-67
Renault, 126
Roffey Park Management Institute, 78
Romaro, Joe, 51
Roney, Alex, 38
Rubio, Janet, 72
Rush, Jonathan, 105

Sampson, Eleri, 12
Sanders, Christine, 95
Sankey, Michael, 44
Sant, Tom, 51
Scannell, Ed, 84
Shapiro, Ron, 103
Shipley Associates, 53
Simon and Schuster, 45
Simons, Christine, 95
Sobel, Andrew, 112
Society of Competitive Intelligence Professionals, The, 45
Stevens, Michael, 13
Still Point, The, 108
Stone, Merlin, 19, 27, 66, 73, 113, 132
SWOT, 41
Syrett, Michel, 78

Taylor, Bob, 98
tender documents, 33-40
Tenders Electronic Daily, 39
Tepper, Ron, 52
Thompson, Harvey, 19
Trade Partners UK, 128
Tradewinds Negotiation Training, 108
Training Solutions, 14
Trompenaars, Fons, 126

TRT, 14
Tweedley, Neil, 28, 31, 32, 38, 90, 105

UK Recruiter, 101
Underwood, J, 44
Unilever, 16
United Biscuits, 59
United Nations, 33
United Nations Development Business, 40
Ury, William, 106

Vause, Bob, 45
Video Arts, 12
Volvo, 126

Walker, Kevin, 112
Ward, Patricia Biedermann, 95
Weiss, Alex, 73, 85, 106
Weissman, Jerry, 12
Wendy Warr & Associates, 47
Whatmore, John, 78
Whiteley, Richard, 26
Willson, Stephen, 73, 85, 106
Wilson, Dr Alan, 19
Wilson, Charles, 112
Woodcock, Neil, 66
World Bank Group, 36
Wyburd, Giles, 126